What's in a Name? Everything!

Heritage   Pride   Uniqueness
Love   Joy
MY STORY
Tradition   Frustration
Confusion   Embarrassment

COMPILED AND EDITED BY
SUSAN CHEEVES KING

Broken Arrow, OK

Scripture quotations marked ESV are taken from The Holy Bible, English Standard Version. ESV® Text Edition: 2016. Copyright © 2001 by Crossway Bibles, a publishing ministry of Good News Publishers. Used by permission. All rights reserved.

Scripture quotations marked NIV are taken from the *The Holy Bible, New International Version.* Copyright © 1973, 1978, 1984, International Bible Society. Used by permission of Zondervan. All rights reserved.

Scripture quotations marked NKJV are taken from the *New King James Version*®. Copyright © 1982 by Thomas Nelson. Used by permission. All rights reserved.

Scripture quotations marked NRSV are taken from the *New Revised Standard Version Bible,* copyright © 1989 the Division of Christian Education of the National Council of the Churches of Christ in the United States of America. Used by permission. All rights reserved.

Royalties for this book are donated to World Christian Broadcasting.

What's in a Name" Everything!
ISBN-13: 978-1-60495-081-6

Copyright © 2022 by Susan King. Published in the USA by Grace Publishing House. All rights reserved. No part of this book may be reproduced in any form or by any electronic or mechanical means, including information storage and retrieval systems, without permission in writing, except as provided by USA Copyright law.

Table of Contents

Introduction 5
1. *The Last First* ~ Susan Engebrecht 7
2. *Names Have Weight* ~ Leah Hinton 10
3. *Grandpa's Front Porch* ~ Rita Klundt 13
4. *X Marks the Spot* ~ Xavia Sheffield 15
5. *From Pain to Peace* ~ Julie Payne 18
6. *First Impressions* ~ S.E. Pruitt 21
7. *Dancing with the River* ~ Kenneth Avon White 23
8. *What Counts* ~ Debra Kornfield 26
9. *Jesus and Angels* ~ Susan Brehmer 28
10. *Hubbard's the Name* ~ Allyson West Lewis 29
11. *No Boy Is Billie Joy* ~ Billie Joy Langston 31
12. *Name Rules* ~ Kelly Godzwa 33
13. *What a Beautiful Name!* ~ Yolando Cooksey 35
14. *King of Peace* ~ William Oliver Sanner Jr. 38
15. *Honor in a Namesake* ~ Suzanne D. Nichols 39
16. *Clear as Glass* ~ Desiree St. Clair Glass 41
17. *Mary Frances* ~ Mary Heitzman 44
18. *I Am Ree* ~ Shelley Pierce 46
19. *That's Not My Real Name* ~ Patty Barry 48
20. *A Wee Orph* ~ Frank Caudle 50
21. *What's Your Name?* ~ Doris Hoover 52
22. *Elizabeth Ann* ~ Liz Kimmel 53
23. *A Girl of Many Names* ~ Martha Rogers 56
24. *By Any Other Name* ~ Wilma Vernich 58
25. *What My Name Isn't* ~ Candice Weathers 60
26. *Hurricane Bob* ~ Jeanne Roberson 63
27. *The Namesake* ~ Gene C. Burgess 66

28. *Thank You for Your Service* ~ Terry Magness 69
29. *A Unique Name* ~ Linda L. Kruschke 71
30. *Little Angelia's Gonna Sing* ~ A. DiAnne Wilson 73
31. *The Name Game* ~ Susan Cheeves King 74
32. *Seventh Time's the Charm* ~ Penny Hunt 78
33. *Where Have You Gone, Joe DiMaggio?* ~ Diana DiMaggio 81
34. *Jud the Jud I* ~ Judson I. Stone 83
35. *Just Jill* ~ Jill Maisch 85
36. *Called by Name* ~ Verdia Yvonne Conner 87
37. *Let Me Count the Ways* ~ Glenda Ferguson 89
38. *No, My Dad Did Not Want a Boy* ~ Kevin Louise Schaner 91
39. *Names I Have Known* ~ Mary Alice Archer 93
40. *The Same Name!* ~ Cristina Moore 95
41. *The Top Ten Things About Being John Leatherman* ~
    John Leatherman 98
42. *The One Who Called My Name* ~ Kellie Zeigler 100
43. *Not Me!* ~ Penny Cooke 103
44. *My Name to Claim* ~ Barbara Farland 105
45. *Lucky Dog* ~ Lin Daniels 108
46. *A Name That Fits* ~ Alice H. Murray 109
47. *The Only M* ~ Mary Lou Redding 112
48. *a boy named ed* ~ Ed Sanabia 115
49. *Oh, for a Name's Sake!* ~ Jorja Davis 116
50. *Lover of Peac*e ~ Rhonda Dragomir 119
51. *The Title I Adore* ~ Becky Alexander 121
52. *Not Short and Not Sweet* ~ Jean Matthew Hall 123
53. *Take His Name* ~ Patricia Tiffany Morris 126

About the Authors 128
Acknowledgment 155

Introduction

What's in a Name?
 Actually, quite a bit. Since they're the first thing we own — and not easy to unload — our names play a huge role in our lives, for better or for worse.

Sometimes the culprit is the first name. In college, my linguistics teacher told of a Ugandan boy who was a troublemaker in every area of his life, especially school. After exhausting other possible solutions to help him, they tried changing his unpleasant-sounding name to one of the Luganda words for *love*. It transformed his life.

We all know of other times when parents haven't been kind in giving names to their offspring. (Ima Hogg rose above her name to become one of the most respected women in Texas during the 20th century.) But sometimes it's unintentional. One friend's parents couldn't decide on a girl's name — even after she was born. Finally, as her father was leaving the hospital room to go fill out the birth certificate, her mother just flippantly said, "I don't care. We can just call her Pebbles." That's the name she still wears today.

And we like to poke fun at even the ordinary names of others — be they first or last.

This especially relates to dating couples. My friends and I spent way too much time imagining what one particular couple might have said on parting at the dorm door: "Good night, Goodnight," with the reply, "'Night, Knight." And we relished our take on the usual punch line of a popular game: "If Sharon Wilson married Kenny Wilson, she'd be Sharon Wilson." She did, and she is.

Needless to say, her name coupling didn't pose any inconvenience. Not so with others. Consider the married name of my first boyfriend's mother: Vannah Vannoy. Then there's the story that well-known Christian writer Sarah Young once told me about her recently married sister, Emily. Sensing a slight problem with Emily's new name, her fiancé had early on worked out a way to handle it — at least during the honeymoon when meeting Christians at churches they planned to visit on the trip: "Hi! I'm Steve Lemley, and this is my wife, Emily." Unfortunately, he said it wrong every time: "Hi! I'm Steve, and this is my wife, Emily Lemley." Rarely did Steve find *himself* in that awkward predicament. Emily's the one who — during now over fifty years of marriage — had to learn to live with it.

Those who entered our country at Ellis Island did have a chance to change their names for reasons ranging from convenience to self-preservation. But too often, the official who was recording the name heard it wrong and thus saddled a family with the wrong name — or at least the wrong spelling. (See "What's Your Name?" on p. 52.)

Others can only wish they'd had a chance to change their name. So, as you might expect, though most people are content with the names they have, a majority of the writers in this book either really love or really hate their names.

But all of us would agree with one take on this theme: As Christians, we wear the name of Christ, and what's in that name is everything. (See 1 Peter 4:16.)

Beyond writing to a certain theme, this book's authors were required to write in a short-and-sweet style.

Like the others before it, Book 10 in the *Short and Sweet* series is based on an assignment I've been giving writers at conferences for over twenty-five years when I teach them about learning to write with excellent style: "Write about something close to your heart using words of only one syllable."

I allow the writers seven exceptions to the one-syllable-word-only requirement. If you see a polysyllabic word in any of these stories, it is because that word fits into one of those exceptions.

If you're a writer — or aspire to be — and the challenge of writing in words of (mostly) one syllable intrigues you, why not give it a try? Contact me at shortandsweettoo@gmail.com to obtain the upcoming themes and deadlines. You could be seeing your own work featured in the next book in the *Short and Sweet* series.

1

The Last First

Susan Engebrecht

With a last name like Peterson, the males in our family had little need for a first name. Even though my dad and uncles did have first names; their wives, co-workers, and friends all called every one of them *Pete*.

Mom, a huge movie fan, named me after Susan Hayward. She even kept a glamour shot of her in my baby book. But Great Grandma Susan told anyone who would listen that I was named in *her* honor. So from early on, Mom made me swear to keep the Susan Hayward link a secret. On the sly I used to sneak a peek at Susan's image in that baby book. Her looks were a high bar — too high for tomboy me.

Early on, I fell to the same fate as the males in the family when most folks, except Mom, dropped Susan and began to call me "Little Pete" or "RePete." A few used "Susie Pete," but most of the time I was just plain Pete. For me, the name was an easy fit, as cozy as the cowboy boots I wore.

Then the teen years hit.

Like most kids, I found life in high school to be a bit dicey and not so comfy in many areas, such as when I had to trade my boots for high heels. Now in a wider world than grade school, I met two who shared my name. One was a guy with the first name Pete, the other with the last name Peters. Like it or not, we became the three Petes of Lincoln High.

Our history teacher liked to stare at the chalk in his hand or the tip of his shoe and say something like, "Pete, answer review question twelve on page fifty-three."

Pete who? Pete would look at me. I'd look at Peters. We would all shrug. The class would laugh. I'm not sure how much history from that class still lives in my head, but the sound of mirth from my peers has stayed with me.

As I look back, I see that what I learned from those years was: Don't take yourself too seriously. Learn to laugh and accept being laughed at. A sack full of laughter makes life more joy-filled and a lot less stressful.

On the day I said "I do," Susie Pete put on the name robe of her knight in faded jeans and began a new trip down the road. In a blink and a dash, fifty years flew by all too fast. Our two boys grew into men, husbands, and fathers.

Last year, Knight and I got news that we were about to be great-grandparents. Joy and queries filled our hearts during the wait.

"What names are they thinking about?" read a text to my son.

"They won't say," came the reply.

Great-Grandma got in a flap. "Won't say?"

"Won't say," I read again in my son's new text.

"Just between you and me," I declared with a wink at Knight, "I'm going to call the baby Peter. After all, *Pete* can be a boy or girl, as I can well attest. Until we hear different, the baby shall be called Peter, at least in this house. Agree? Is this family secret okay with you?" With a grin and a nod, Knight sealed the pact.

At last the day came — with a text that the baby was here. And a photo.

"Will you tell us a name now?" I sent back.

"Peter James." The news made me gasp. I sat down fast — and let the secret out. I told our grandson the name I had given his son before his birth.

Knight and I have met Peter, heard his laugh, and felt the grip of his tiny hand. We love him even more each day.

The first time the Joy-Boy of my heart and I were alone, I said into his ear in a soft voice, "My last name has become your first name. Wear the name Peter well."

2

Names Have Weight

Leah Hinton

Names have weight. Ever since I heard the Hebrew sense of *Leah* — "weary" and "weak-eyed" — I have not liked my name. Also, from her role in the Old Testament the name has seemed to mean "less-than."

Few have been able to say my name right when they read it. To me, it seems easy. Four letters. Two syllables. Lee-uh. If I could read and write my name as a mere child, why couldn't adults do the same? When paired with my birth name, *Polvado*, my whole name was a maze few could get through.

No teacher ever said Leah right on the first day of any grade-school year — even when I made a point to shake hands and say it first. This error with my name was one thing I could count on.

I've been called Lee, which I get.

I've been called Leia (Lay-uh), which I also get and rather like as I wore my hair in buns on the sides of my head for years, just like the Star Wars princess.

I've even been called LeeAnne. I don't know where that one comes from. It's as if others think I spell my own name wrong, so they add the *n* for me.

Fourth grade is a hard year in any girl's life. But I had so much more going on. This was the same year that, time after time, my birth father — who had no part in my life — would thwart my stepdad's efforts to adopt me. After many failed tries, my stepdad moved to have my name changed in the courts since adoption was not on the table.

I was a bit sad as a child. I had often felt as if I did not fit in. So, this name change was a big deal. It meant so much to my young heart to have my stepdad's last name. It was in the spring of my fourth-grade year when my last name changed to his. He was my dad-dad now.

Amid the chaos, I had a kind math teacher named Mrs. Gilbert. She was round, jolly, and soft for hugs. This woman made you smile. I don't know now, as an adult who looks back, if it was dyslexia that gave her pause when it came to my name, or if she thought it was cute, but she called me "Leehaw" for the bulk of the school year. Think L-e-h-a not L-e-a-h.

Mrs. Gilbert thought Leehaw's name change was the best thing in my nine years of life. I was now a *Lobb*. Leehaw Lobb. But she couldn't leave it there. She clapped her hands and said, "Leehaw, you are a wee lobster now." Thus was my nickname born. My class called me "Lobster." Leehaw Lobster. At times it felt like a jab, but I knew Mrs. Gilbert's heart was in a good place. To have a nickname can be a cool thing even if it's from your teacher and not your peers. But what is the weight of Leehaw?

On the Lobb side of my family your nickname is made of the first letter of your first name plus "Lobb." Uncle Greg was "Globb." My new dad was "Klobb." And my poor Grandpa Bill was "Blobb." In that light, Lobster was A-Okay. What is the weight of Lobster? Or worse, what is the weight of Klobb?

I finished out fourth grade and went through most of fifth grade as Lobster. That year, my mom told me I was going to be a big sister. My whole family came up with names, then chose *Rachel*. If you know the Bible story of Leah and Rachel, the very last name I'd ever have chosen for my sister is Rachel. I didn't want to be the big sister who was the butt of a joke, the one who wasn't wanted. To this day I don't know if my parents ever knew how big of a deal this was for me. I felt as if my joy in life hung on their choice. As luck would have it, my dad was a huge fan of *The Bob Newhart Show* and thus their choice changed to *Suzanne* after Suzanne Pleshette.

My poor kid brain was on fire with hope. I felt that I had gained a new chance.

My teen years had less Lobster and next to zero Leehaw. I was even Leah for a bit. By 12th grade, Lobster picked back up among my peers and that was okay. It was a name I'd grown-up with. And it was a easy thing to live with. (My poor sister Suzanne was "Slobb." When I think about what Slobb would weigh, Lobster was easy!)

As an adult I wed a Hinton. Even he called me Lobster. As an author, I didn't know how my name should read on a book. History was proof that my name is hard to read. If I had a web page such as leahhinton.com, would people be able to spell it? When I did a web search for my name, I found there were a slew of realtors named Leah Hinton, and a jazz singer who had rights to most of the Leah Hinton sites out there. I had no idea there were so many of us! I thought I could drop Hinton and use Leah Michelle. That would work, right? But there is an actress who has the rights to Lea Michele. In the end, I chose *LM Hinton*. A person would have to have a lit mind to think of SE Hinton, which is a name I would like to live up to in terms of being an author.

I have since found a new truth to the name Leah. The name I was told means weary and weak eyed doesn't mean that at all. Not to me. Leah of the Bible was strong. Life sprung from her, which stilled her tears.

My life proves my name has weight. Love, light, and life.

But truth be told, it might have been easier to sign all my work Leehaw Lobster.

3

Grandpa's Front Porch

Rita Klundt

My mother had only two names, her first and last.

"Why?" the six year-old me asks.

"With a name like *Ellene*, she doesn't need more than two names," Grandpa says.

"But your name is *Garvis* and you have three names!"

"So I do."

Most of the time, Grandpa had words to spare but not on that theme, that day, and not after a big meal. We sat on the front porch and talked, not out loud, but in my dreams — day dreams.

He tells me how much he loves me and that I am as cute as a bug in a rug. He brags that I am sweet and quite smart. I tell him he is the best grandpa ever.

Just the two of us. The taste of peach pie still on our lips. Life is good on Grandpa's porch. We watch cars go by and wave. My waves are big. His right fingers lift, but his palm stays fixed to his knee. A dog barks, and I see a horse in the field on the other side of the road.

"Can I ride him?"

"The dog?"

"No, Grandpa. The horse!"

"He's not our horse, and he's a she."

"But can I ride her?"

"She's old."

"But can I ride her?"

"No."

I go back to my day dream. Grandpa's eyes are on me, and he smiles. His lips don't move, but I hear him say how much he likes for me to sit with him.

"Grandpa doesn't know how to play with girls," Grandma told me one time. The grandchildren he sees all the time are boys. Aunt Lou's boys like to chase and stir up dust. This time of day, Grandpa likes to sit. Me too.

The front porch is nice. We're in the shade, and the hot July sun is on its way to the other side of the world.

"I like these chairs," I say. "Yours squeaks."

Grandpa stares. His head doesn't turn.

"Dad has oil in the trunk of the car."

I know to wait and not push for words. How I know, I can't say, but I think I wait long enough.

"I like my names. All three of them," I say.

One edge of Grandpa's lips turns up. That's all.

"Is it too late to give Mom a middle name?"

I think *June would be nice. Or Mary.*

It's a dumb thought, and Grandpa tells me so, but only with a deep sigh. The screen door swings out and Mom is there.

"Did I hear my name?" She looks to me first, then Grandpa.

He clears his throat with a grunt. His thumb slips into a belt loop and he speaks. "This chair squeaks. Needs some oil."

Mom says, "Howard keeps oil in the trunk."

"Rita told me." Grandpa winks so that Mom can't see.

My chest swells.

So good were the sights and sounds from Grandpa's front porch.

4

X Marks the Spot

Xavia Sheffield

Would you reply to "Hey, X?" For most of my life, I have.
When I was born, I was given the name *Diana Xavia Arndt*. My father chose Diana; my mother, Xavia. She told me she took Xavier, a man's name, and changed the *i-e-r* to *i-a* at the end. The right way to say my name would be *Zavia* in the same way that xylophone is "zylophone." But my mother called me *X-avia* with the *X* sound and then a break from the *X* to the *avia*. I had that name until my parents split up when I was five years old.

My mother, whom my brothers and I lived with, then chose to say my name as if it were spelled Z-a-v-i-a. She liked it more. She once told me she thought about a name change to Cynthia, since she liked that too.

I also got a name change to Diane from Diana. My legal name is now Xavia Diane and shows up that way on my Social Security card and other ID's. But, when the lady at the DMV in the state of Virginia saw my birth certificate with Diana Xavia on it, she did not want to issue me a card. Still, I got one in the end.

I have been called by a lot of names. Close family call me just plain X, or Xie (X-E). Other friends and family have pet names for me. One cousin calls me "Cugat," after Xavier Cugat, the man who led in the spread of Latin music. Often that cousin just says, "Cugie." I laugh. One friend calls me Xave (Zave). An aunt called me Axy! And an uncle called me Xus (X-us). I don't know where he got that. One uncle gave up on the whole thing and called me Maude. I never did ask him about that. None, I guess, knew quite what to do with my name!

I have been called Xavi-er at least as often as I have been called Xav-ia. A few who've known me for many years still call me Xavier. I have been sent dozens of pieces of mail to Mr. or Mrs. Xavier Arndt or Sheffield, my married name. A few were sent to Zavia. One day I got a letter to Zxavia. I guess they put in both the Z and the X to make sure. And my gas bill still says, Xazia. There is no form on the bill for a name change! Once, to be cute, (or so I thought) I signed my name on a line as *avia*, using the X on the line to show where to sign as the first-letter in my name. After that, I got mail sent to *avia*. I should've known.

When some say, "I love that name" or "That is so pretty," I just reply, "Thank You." It makes me feel good when they say my name right or get it right on the first try. I am happy with those who take the time to ask me about it when they see it on a name tag and don't just stare and walk away.

Most often, I am asked, "How do you say that?" or "Spell it for me."

But there is also a down side to having such a rare name. To live with an odd name can be hard on a child. The name Xavia made me shy and timid. I got teased and laughed at; I felt out of place. I would turn red and look down when I heard it.

In grade school, when I learned cursive writing, I could never get the large X right. It was all curly and hard to write. I still don't use it.

In high school, I felt like the whole Algebra class tried to "solve" me ($x + y = ?$) But as much as they tried, no one could. (My husband still says I can't be solved!)

In grad school, I had a hard time with my identity, too. It was the 1970s and we were all into "I Gotta Be Me." But who was

Me? When I worked in New York City in the 1970s, some of the men got a kick out of calling me Xaviera, after the former Dutch call girl and madam, Xaviera Hollander, who wrote the hit book, *The Happy Hooker.* What could I do? It was also in New York that I met a girl from South America with my name — the only one ever.

On the fun side, I could be the CEO of Brand X! Or have a chic threads line called XAVIA; or a skin care line called the X-Factor. I could open a baked goods shop called "BakeX." The *X-Files* could be the name of my blog. I could even be a super hero — with X-ray vision, of course! Or, last but not least, I could make a film called *Xavia with an X.* After all, the title of Liza Minelli's 1972 concert film was *Liza with a "Z"!*

Often I have wished my name were more usual. It seems to have taken me my whole life to get used to it. And yes, I have had some fun with it, but in a way, it still doesn't feel quite right.

One thing did come from it, though. I gave my children more usual names.

Maybe Cynthia would have been best after all. But then I would be called "Cindy," or would it be "Cin" for short? I can hear it now — the first day the school kids make a taunt about *Sin.* I guess all names have their issues.

5
From Pain to Peace

Julie Payne

With his blonde hair and blue eyes, my dad may not have looked Italian, but his last name gave him away. So to avoid anti-Italian bias, early in his life he changed his last name from *Piantedosi* to *Payne*. Why Payne? I hold on to the idea that he felt akin to the famed jazz musician Cecil Payne. Both Cecil and my dad played the saxophone and both were born in Brooklyn, New York — and only nine years apart.

While this new last name pleased my dad, it proved a real pain to me. I learned the hard way about mean kids and those who bully. I was often mocked and made fun of in school. Kids teased me: "Julie, Julie, what a pain. Send her away on a plane."

All my self-doubts found birth in those eleven words. They stung deep and seared into my mind. The shame and hurt they caused me lodged in my heart for years. I held on to those words and beat myself up with them. I had no joy in who I was or what I did and made it my life's goals to please, to be loved, and to *not* be a pain.

***

At the age of thirty, I had a nasty split with my live-in boyfriend that left my heart sick, and soul crushed. After a very long pity party, I had just about cried myself to sleep when I had a one-on-one visit from Jesus that changed my life.

Alone in a room, on what should have been flowered curtains, I saw the face of Jesus with a long beard and a crown of thorns. Right next to Him was the face of Satan with gaunt cheeks and sharp horns. In the midst of them were two white eyes as if God stared right at me.

My own eyes were fixed on the whole image in front of me. *How could this be? Why is this here?* In all my pain, the thought of God had not once crossed my mind. After I'd stared and probed for some time, God spoke to my heart.

"Julie, you need to make a decision here."

All it took was for me to say, "I choose you, Jesus!" At once, I felt peace flood my soul; a peace I had never felt. It swept through me from my head to my toes. In less than a blink of an eye my heart changed. My point of view changed. My life changed. The deep hurts of all the years fled! There was now only pure peace; from God to me, and from me to all those who had scorned me.

God sought me in my need, even though I had not searched for Him.

Isaiah 65:1 (NKJV) tells us, *"I was sought by those who did not ask for Me; I was found by those who did not seek Me. I said, 'Here I am, here I am,' To a nation that was not called by My name."*

God reached down to me and laid a new path for my life. I read God's Word as if starved. The more I read the Bible, the more I felt His great love for me. I admit, the pain in my heart had caused me to give up on God; but He never gave up on me. That day, He sought me when I had not looked for Him. That is how much He loves me. That is how much He loves all of us and wants to bring peace to our lives.

* * *

One Sunday, my pastor said he hoped to ask some to share at a night of praise what God had done for them. I had a great deal to share and I did not want to wait to be asked, or worse, not be asked at all. So, I asked him if I could speak. He looked stunned. "Are you kidding?"

"No, not at all. I want to tell my story. I didn't want you to ask others and not give me a chance. I'd love to speak. Can you find a spot for me? Please?"

After what seemed like a long time, he gave me a nod and said, "Sure."

Then came the night of praise. The pastor went to the podium. "Good evening church. Are you ready to be blessed? We have several members who have agreed to speak tonight, but I want to start the night with someone who asked me if she could speak. Over the many years that we have done these praise and testimony nights, no one — I say no one — has ever come to me wanting to stand up here and speak."

He smiled and faced the area I sat in. "But she insisted until I agreed. She had purposed in her heart to share her testimony, and I applaud her for that. Without further ado, I would like to introduce her to you. Here is a lady who is a Payne through and through." The crowd laughed at the pun. "I recently found out her middle name is Ann. And that confirmed what I already knew. Church, may I introduce to you, Julie . . . A . . . Payne."

Again, the crowd laughed and clapped. I laughed too and walked up to the podium. Right then, I knew that God had truly healed me as He filled me once again with His peace. No hurt arose from my pastor's joke. My name and all that went with it in the past were now fully freed from pain. As I shared my story, I knew in my heart that God was pleased. His peace had taken away my pain.

He has changed my life, and for that I give Him all the glory.

6

First Impressions

S.E. Pruitt

"How old are you, Sarah?"

When I was a child the only ones who called me *Sarah* worked at Kaiser Hospital. Sarah is my legal name and was that way on all my hospital files. Every time before she'd give me a shot, the nurse would ask my age — not that she didn't know, but just to take my mind off the prick.

I don't know how my parents chose my name. After I was born, my mother found out that my dad's great-grandmother was named Sarah. My paternal grandmother was thrilled at their name choice, but it was just a coincidence. Too bad. She would have been a great person to be named for. What a lady! She learned to read as an adult while her husband was off fighting in the Civil War.

I was born three wars and one-hundred-thirteen years after her. By that time, the name had gone out of style.

The only other Sarah I knew about was the evil aunt in Disney's *Lady and the Tramp*. In the face of this truth, I could see that life as I knew it would be over should my real name be known. I'm a firstborn, and am teased for being bossy. I was *not* going through life being called "Aunt Sarah." So, I kept Sarah a secret.

It wasn't hard. Few knew my real name since my parents called me "Sally." So, I was Sally in four towns and three schools. I could live with that name in spite of the kid chant that started, "When

Sally was a baby . . ." (baby being a four-letter word in third grade) and, of course, that Erie Canal song about a mule named Sal. Since these did no lasting harm I began high school as Sally.

In the sixties, some college students took part in protests and riots. My great act of defiance took place late summer of 1967.

I had just flunked my second try to pass my driver's test. Still, I lived in hope that one day I would pass. And I did not want to go through life with a nickname on my license.

So, I marched into the bank, the library, and my high school's front office and had *Sally* changed to *Sarah*. Then, I waited, thrilled, for this new phase of life to begin.

It wasn't what I thought it would be. The first time I said, "Here," when the teacher called out, "Sarah," I felt a vast sense of loss. (I can be a drama queen.) It felt as if I had closed a door and not found a new one to open.

My family found the change hard. My dad died thirty-six years later. Until the last, when he said Sarah, I could hear a tiny pause when I'm sure his brain said Sally first. My mom said Sarah as though she wasn't sure it was the right name. (She had six children, so at times couldn't keep the names straight.) My five siblings made more of an effort.

After graduation, I got a teaching job and moved to a new town. I loved teaching and made friends with other teachers. I joined a new church and found more friends. All call me Sarah.

Today most of my close friends know me as Sarah. My nieces and nephews call me Auntie Sarah. Sally was a lovely nickname, but Sarah is my name. I just had to grow into it.

One day, as some of my nieces and nephews sat down to watch *Lady and the Tramp*, I heard one of their parents say, "The Aunt Sarah in this movie is mean. Not like our Aunt Sarah."

As it turns out, I don't mind being called Aunt Sarah after all.

7

Dancing with the River

Kenneth Avon White

When I'm in a group and the talk makes me want to take a nap, one of the thoughts that might pop up deals with the love-hate polka I've danced with my middle name.

When I was a young teen, I had an aunt who, when not pleased with me, hailed me using my first and middle name. She'd squeal, "Kenneth AAAvonnnn" — my middle name drawn out so I would feel the full weight of the bad deed. Each time, I would cringe with a bit of shame. To most folks the name *Avon* brought to mind lipstick, eye liner and sprays with elfin scents. That's tough on a boy from Texas where young men chewed nails to get fired up for a Friday night game or had cool names like *Gunner*, *Butch* or *Tanner*. That's why early on I hid my middle name under a rock and kept a box of nails handy to fit in.

Then David, my soon-to-be best friend came along. David taught me the power of a known name. Texas had many of those – Mary Kay Ash of Mary Kay Cosmetics, the Hunts who could sail a fleet on their sea of oil and DeBakey who gave more new hearts to those with frail ones than Texas has boots. That's when I began to think, *What would my life be like if I were part of the clan that brought us the beauty brand Avon?*

A glimpse into David's roots gives a clue as to why he had a lust for things grand. He lived in Houston's fifth ward in a house held up with Duct tape. This ward was about as far from Shangri-La as you could get. By day one could see all the dross of the bad things done at night. My home and hood was not as dire, but I did have friends drop me off two blocks down the street. We both had a goal to break out as fast as we could. At that point in our lives all we could do is flee for a few hours and try to mimic the life of the uber rich in some weird, proxy kind of way.

The thing of it is our war chest would not even cover their cost to have a dog groomed. So, our quest to dress right, talk right, and be seen at the right place at the right time began with some tricky moves. We shopped at thrift stores near River Oaks — Houston's millionaire mile — in search of shirts and pants by Ralph Lauren. We made a point to be seen at spots with flair — like at a posh brunch (via coupons) or a swank horse show (snuck into through the woods next to the River Oaks Country Club). If asked, I was Avon White — an heir to the Avon cosmetics line.

For years I whirled around the dance floor of my life with this faux sense of self. Truth be told, I was far from being one with no lack, and the act got hard to keep up. I mean, my car shook as I drove, and sounds boomed out of the back. After college it was time to grow up. The polka stopped. I set the name *Avon* to rest. The more adult Kenneth White was the name I was known by for years.

Then my faith in God rose from the dead. With this sense of new life came a dream to write about ideas, plots, and past trials caged in my head.

That's when I heard strains of polka music begin again.

I need to write under a name other than Kenneth White, I thought. *That name is void of zing or bling. It's a name to be tacked to a study or white paper. I need a name that leaps into the path of those who traipse down the aisles of Barnes & Noble.*

I kicked that can down the road for a long time. *I could make up a pen name.* But for me that choice felt like a mask one puts on at Halloween. Then, my plight got real. I learned of a chance to have a short piece put in print. *I need a sign from above.* The angst got thick.

The next thing I knew signs began to rain down like bricks. and I got hit by one that tripped a wire in this old bean of mine.

In school, a phrase had often popped up when my study of playwrights was at its peak: William Shakespeare from Stratford-Upon-Avon. Each time I heard it, my ears would perk up. Turns out Stratford, England, the place where Shakespeare was born, is situated on the River Avon.

Shakespeare is an icon and my middle name is tied to him, I mused.

I also learned the word Avon means "river" or "the river." Some of the Bible verses I like the most use the image of a river to make a point — such as Revelation 22:1: *"He showed me a pure river of water of life, clear as crystal, proceeding from the throne of God and of the Lamb"* (NKJV).

When I joined these two points, the dance with my middle name came to an end. I had learned that the name Avon is not a thing to hide from, nor use toward a false goal. It is a name in step with real things I hold dear. Who could ask for more?

8

What Counts

Debra Kornfield

In nurse garb, I enter the lift. A man stares at my name tag. "Is that your birth name or your married name?" he asks.

"It's my married name."

"You sure must have loved that guy," he says as he exits.

That guy is Dave Kornfield, whose mother once told me their last name is German for "a field of wheat."

"Think of lovely golden grain, rippling in a breeze," she said. "Think of Jesus' story: the good seed, the good soil, the abundant crop. Be good soil. Be proud to bear a bountiful crop."

Google says that the field-of-wheat name is *Kornfeld*, not Kornfield. But that's okay since Dave's aunt said her dad's name was Kornfeld when he lived in Russia. On Ellis Island he added the "i" to flee the shame of the pogroms. "He did it to save us from what he suffered," she told me. My brother-in-law tried to change back to Kornfeld when he wed, but Aunt Helen got so upset that he just gave it up.

My daughter-in-law likes the name. She thinks it's a hoot.

"Kornfield, with a *K*" comes easy to me now. But it wasn't always like this. At first, I got mad. When most folks first hear the name, they reply, "Spell it."

I sigh. "Write cornfield, but start with a *K*."

"Spell it."

I sigh. "***K***-o-r-n-f-i-e-l-d." And still, they write it with a *C*.

"Let me do it for you," I beg.

Our daughter Karis, after days of the chant "Karis Kornfield who lives in a cornfield" by the child in the hospital bed next to hers, made up a game. "Be quiet for one minute. Me too. I'll time us. Good job! Now let's try two minutes."

Since 1990 when we started mission work in Brazil, the folks there have had a hard time when they try to say our name. "Kornifieldgy," they say, with the *d-g* sound as in judge. And then the usual extra *e-e* sound they add to hard ends.

"It feels like they are mocking us," I said at first. "Let's use only first names." Often, we could. But Dave's name then came out "Davidgy."

"It sounds like a baby name," I griped. "Davidgy Kornifieldgy. Say that ten times fast."

"Here's what counts: They love us," said Dave.

And they do.

9

Jesus and Angels

Susan Brehmer

My first name is *Susan*, a name I share with many of my friends. When I was small, I wished I had a name that seemed less plain. Even though some called me "Susie," I still knew many with that name. One friend called me "Suse," which was not my name at all. After the boy who lived across the street lost his two front teeth, his new lisp changed my name to "Sooth." Funny that. So many ways to miss the true name I had been given.

Still I wished for my real name to be one that stood out, not one so bland. I hoped for one that was a gift, that showed a bit of flair, but didn't know how to find it.

Until one day I saw a sign. In Sunday School the teacher wrote of Jesus and angels. In fact, those three words were all that graced that piece of stiff paper board tacked up on the wall. I looked once, then looked again. I began to stare at the words at the front of the room until what I saw was not only "Jesus and angels," but me as well — my name right next to both Jesus and those hosts of heaven. "Je*sus an*d angels." Now I knew that my name was a gift. Jesus and His friends sat on either side of me — at least for as long as I watched from in front of their sign.

I liked the sign so much that I asked the teacher if I could take it home. And she gave it to me! The sign hung in our kitchen for as long as I can recall. Each time I sat at the table to eat or do school work, I glanced up and saw my name on the wall right there with Jesus and angels.

My name is Susan. A good name to have after all.

10

Hubbard's the Name

Allyson Lewis

> Old Mother Hubbard
> Went to the cupboard,
> To fetch her poor dog a bone;
> When she got there,
> The cupboard was bare,
> And so the poor dog had none.

Alas, at school, cool kids rule and will 'til the cows come home. As a child, I never could fit into cool-kid mold. Bright white scars ran up and down my legs and one of my arms. Mean kids would tease and taunt me and leave my poor heart maimed.

Then my friends found out that one of the names I bore — my middle name — was *Hubbard*. When kids think of Hubbard, they also think of the rhyme, Old Mother Hubbard — which stirred glee in the pack of mean girls and boys since it gave them one more weapon in our one-sided war.

In eighth grade, my parents sent me to a school where the kids had to wear uniforms. Even in the heat of mid-Florida, I cheered to wear knee socks and tops that hid my scars. In a snap, even though I was still a shy girl, I was also a whole girl.

By then, the Old Mother Hubbard taunts had died out. And around that same time, I found out that Hubbard had been the last name of my grandmother.

Time passed, and when I wed, I left the name of Hubbard back in my youth. For many long years, I did not miss it at all.

Now, it seems hard to recall why that grand name grieved me so. Since the name is part of my family lore, I chose to dig for the gist of it.

The true sense of that name fills me with joy. Like most names, Hubbard comes from more than one place. In one sense, it means "heart, mind, and spirit" which can stand for love and smarts.

One source of the name is "fame" — never an aim of mine. But with it comes a sense of "bright," which was like my mother's kind light that has been a true foil of dark nights.

And the last sense of Hubbard is "fight" or "strife." Early in my life, this did not ring true, but it could mean the spunk that later grew in me. Maybe it stands for what I had to go through to find life!

11

No Boy Is Billie Joy

Billie Joy Langston

Like most kids' names, my name is a gift from my parents at birth — and what a great gift it is! From day one, I loved it. For me, being a girl with a boy's name was cool. I liked its sound. And it fit me. From grade school through college, it made me stand out, alone from the pack of other girls.

As a child, I was a tomboy. My world was the open air, where I would ride my bike over rough land on our farm near the Virginia coast. I shared the front seat of our farm truck with Dad and Pop when we took the pigs to sell in Smithfield. I was one-hundred-percent girl, but I was really drawn to "guy" stuff.

Even though Billie as a girl's name was known in the south, not many of us were left in my town when I was in high school in the 1970s. True, Aunt Billie had grown up in the same town, but I had never known her.

She had been my Dad's sister, whose short life ended at the age of twenty-nine in a tragic car crash. Legend has it that Dad wanted another Billie in the family. Even though I could never take her place, I was the lucky one to carry on her name.

Over the years, I'd longed to know more about my aunt. I was able to glean a lot of things from old photos, chats with family, and worn papers kept in my grandmother's family Bible. Aunt Billie liked horses and wore western gear, just like me. She was strong and tough like a guy, but also gentle and kind. Being in the house with dolls was not her forté. Neither was it mine.

Living in my rural town as the lone female Billie of my time didn't slow me down at all. When folks from preachers to teachers tacked *y* vs. *ie* on the end, I was kind to share with them the right way to spell my name. And I found a great way to do it.

"No, it is Billie, like a boy, but I'm not," I say, when a person has spelled my name wrong as "Billy."

The quip was not planned. One day, when I was fifteen, the words just came out of my mouth and have stuck for well over forty years. When I frame my name in this way, I still get smiles and good vibes, no matter what rural town or urban city I'm in. And often, the Billie spell check makes me new friends.

When it came time to name me, my Mom made a deal with Dad. He got to pick Billie as my first name, and she got to choose Joy as my middle name. And this name had a bit of spin as well. Back in the late 1950s when I was born, Proctor and Gamble had ads on TV for a new dish wash soap called Joy. Mom saw the ads while at home waiting for me to be born. She thought it was a great middle name that went well with Dad's choice for first name. So voila! Billie Joy was born. To this day, I still get a kick out of the sight of my middle name on a bottle of the popular dish soap in the store.

From the start, I gave my parents huge kudos for their joint choice of my first and middle names. What's more, Dad earned a super A+ for carrying the Langston last name. Our family's oral history tells of our kinship with Langston Hughes. That fact alone spurs me on in my writing career.

Names are for all time. And my name shaped who I was meant to be. I plan to keep it.

Name Rules

Kelly Godzwa

My Dad liked rules for the names of his kids; my Mom did, too. There must be five letters in each name. That's rule one. The next rule is this: The initials should spell a word or name. They gave me *Kelly Ellyn* with their last name *Yaple* so KEY. Dad has DAY. Mom is KAY. You get it. Years later, my sis would be SKY, and the last child, MAY.

I liked my name and that it was spelled, with a *Y* in all three! (Though at one point when I was eleven or twelve I did try an *i* at the end of *K-e-l-l* so I could dot it with a heart — but that didn't stick.)

Their choice shaped me.

My folks chose what I would be called. What I didn't know was how it would fit with the call of God on my life, the call that took me out of state, out of the U.S., too. When I learned Spanish, my professor keyed in on my name and said that this new language was my key to the hearts of those who spoke it. Now here I am, sixteen years later, bound once more to live and share God's Word in Mexico and give hope to those who have none. I think of that key all the time. With the words I speak, I can open a door that has been locked. Those words need to make sense to the one who hears them. With God's help, I step out in faith on the path He has placed in front of me.

At times, I make my plans, but every time He guides my steps.

When asked where I would *not* want to live, I said, "Where the bugs don't die." Yes, you guessed it. We spent over twelve years at sea level where it's hot all the time!

Math is the class I taught in those early years, not Bible. Yet, it paid the bills that took away the debt and freed us to serve. (Our kids also knew they could go to me for help in school when it came to math!)

Life has a few twists and turns, to be sure, but Jesus doesn't leave my side. (Five letters in His name, too. I didn't think of it when I began to write this piece. Funny, that.)

He may share more keys with me as we go — through His Word, friends, or the stuff of life. KEY began as my name. It then linked with God's call on my life, and now serves to keep my focus on Him as He opens doors I can't.

Thanks be to Him, who knows all and uses all things for our good!

13
What a Beautiful Name!

Yolando Cooksey

On a warm August day in 1959 Houston, Texas — Harris County, Fifth Ward — a baby girl was born. I was given the name *Yolando*.

The usual way to spell this name would be with an *a* on the end since I was a female baby. But my mother wished for my name to stand out. Even the hospital put the wrong name, Yolanda, on my birth certificate. So, I spent most of my childhood, teens, and young-adult years answering to Yolanda, but I wrote my name as Yolando. When asked my name, I would say, "Yolando" and people would say, "That's a male name." I would just shrug and tell them the story my mother told me. Since I was going to be a big baby (over 8 pounds), she felt she might be having twins. She planned for a girl to be named Yolando and a boy to be named Olando. But on the day, it was just me.

In school, when I would tell the teachers my name, they would just look at me as if I had said an alien word. Then, with a half-smile, I would think, *Watch them mess up my name.* I made it through my grade-school years without being teased, which was great. I would cringe when I heard kids make fun of some of the other kids' names, but I was glad they liked mine.

Oddly enough, my father could never say my name right. He chose to call me *Landa*. At times, he would use my nickname, "Pig," given to me since I loved to eat. I was not like some kids, who are very picky about what they eat. If it was on a plate in front of me, I ate it — or at least most of the foods my mother or dad cooked. Later in life, I found out that my birth year is the Year of the Pig on the Chinese calendar. I guess, when Dad gave me that nickname, he knew what he was doing after all.

To me, a person's name is prized. To say someone's name right is vital; it shows the value and worth of the person who wears it. So as I got older, all the years of hearing my name said the wrong way finally took its toll. I would get upset when my name was spelled or spoken wrong, and each time I would correct the person. They would then reply that they were sorry and go on to say my name the right way.

A person's name is with them for all time. Unless they use legal means to change the name given them, they are stuck with it. That's why I took care with the names I chose for my two sons. When I named my first son, I chose the three names to start with T-L-M. To me, it meant "tender loving man" which is exactly what he grew up to be. My baby boy was named after a famous playwright and actor, and this son has the same kind of creative mind. But he was not given a middle name; and to this day, he lets me know I should have given him one.

As an adult, I looked up the meaning of my name and its history. I learned that Yolanda comes from the Spanish for "violet flower" or "purple," and purple is one of my favorite colors. In the *Urban Dictionary*, Yolanda means "a very sweet, kind woman." And I am known as a caring and compassionate woman.

I also learned that Yolando is the male version of Yolanda. This may have touched my life in a couple of ways. First, growing up I was a tomboy. I did not like to wear dresses or frilly clothes, or play much with dolls. On the other hand, being outdoors was and still is my happy place! I love to camp, fish, paint the house, mow the yard, or work on the car with my father.

Yolando also has ties to the Bible. The word purple is found in the Bible forty-eight times. When I learned this and other facts, things all began to make sense to me. I love the Spanish language and foods. I also love the Bible tie to God since I have a heart for Him. I feel blessed to have been given a good name.

The other day, while I was in a store to shop, a lady came up to me and asked my name. After I told her Yolando, she said, "I'm sorry. You're not who I thought you were. By the way, you have a beautiful name. It's different. Who named you?" I shared the story my mother told me, and she smiled. Little did she know that what she'd said about my name had turned my bad day into a very good one. As I made my way toward the check stand, I had pep in my step and a smile from ear to ear. On the way to my car, I thought, *Wow, having a beautiful name sure makes a difference!*

14

King of Peace

William Oliver Sanner, Jr.

My name is William Oliver, and I'm a Junior, which, of course, means that my dad and I shared the same name. I learned how to be a William Oliver from him. He was a great man in life with so much to show for it. In death, his works go on through me.

The name *William* is the name of kings. Noble kings of the past risked their lives for their lands and the folk of the lands. Those folk felt safe due to the king's great deeds. They took pride in him and in fact, loved their king.

My second name, *Oliver*, speaks of the olive tree, which for eons has stood for peace.

When placed side by side, William Oliver means that I'm a hero of sorts — a king of peace. So, what is that about? To me, it means that my dad led and taught me to be a good man and to tell the truth all the time. He spurred me on to lead and to reach out and, in God's strength, change things in my sphere toward the best they can be. This is the life for which I strive.

It all comes down to one word: integrity. I've heard that integrity means doing the right thing even when no one sees you. This is the core of a "king of peace."

Of course, Jesus Christ, the Son of God, is the one true King of Peace. I love Him as the King of kings, and any "king" power I have comes from Him.

Our lives are short. I, William Oliver, want to make mine count. Our world needs more William Olivers, doesn't it?

15

Honor in a Namesake

Suzanne D. Nichols

Deep in thought, I rubbed the cloth over the plate until the dish shone. My mother stood at my side. She held a wet glass over the sink and let it drip as she watched me, aware that I was lost in the strokes of this easy task.

Since she had once been a girl of eight at a sink of dish water with her mother, she didn't scold me for being slow. Girls of eight often dream away the weary tasks in spite of the extra time it takes.

"What's on your mind?" my mother asked.

I set the dish on the rack and took the wet glass from her hand.

"Why did you and Daddy give me such a weird middle name?" I asked as I bunched the cloth into the glass. "Other girls have middle names like Michelle and Lynn and Beth. When my friends ask me my middle name, I just say, 'You will never guess,' and they never do."

Mother dried her hands and leaned on the sink to look at me.

"I guess you're right. *Sibley* is an odd middle name for a girl. But your daddy gave you this name in honor of his great-grandmother. Sibley was her maiden name."

"I'm named for my great-great-grandmother?" I mused as I placed the dry glass on the rack with the other clean items. "Why?"

"Well, Grandmother — as all her folks called her — raised two of her four grandchildren after their mother, her daughter, died in a fire. One of those two children was your grandfather, your daddy's father."

I searched my mother's face as she went on. "You should be proud. Don't you see?"

I did see. In fact, as the years went by, my child-like views were chased away by a sense of honor for my Sibley name. When folks asked about my middle name, I'd spell it out with pride and tell them about my great-great-grandmother.

Later into my adult years, my mother told me of a Sibley cousin she knew I'd bond with if we'd ever met. Our shared love for words in any form drew me to learn more of this cousin — the well-known and much-loved novelist, syndicated columnist, and newspaper reporter for close to sixty of her eighty-five years, Celestine Sibley.

As I delved into the story of Celestine's life, I found that she took a God-given skill and made it her life's work. The same could be said of my great-great-grandmother Helen Sibley, who took her skill as a mother and made it her life's work to raise my grandfather from a baby to a man.

These two women who share the Sibley name with me are like two bright threads stitched and crossed into the woven cloth of my life. Their threads touch my threads in ways that push and pull me to make the most of the skills God has given me as His child, as a woman, and as a lover of words.

Though I never met Helen or Celestine Sibley, they both live with high honor in my heart.

16

Clear as Glass

Desiree St. Clair Glass

I was born Desiree Anne St. Clair. My mother said my first name came from the book *Désirée*. As a teen, she read this true love story about Désirée Clary and Napoleon Bonaparte. She also saw their story play out in a 1954 film by the same title. She fell in love with the name *Desirée* and chose to give it to me, her first daughter.

Per Google, Desiree is pronounced DEH·zr·ay, but I didn't know that as a young child. Most of the time I went by DEH·zr·ee or DEHZ·ree, as my siblings used to say. A cousin called me dehz·RA, which I couldn't stand, but I was too shy to tell her.

One day when the mother of a school mate heard friends call me DEH·zr·ee, she asked, "How do *you* say your name?"

"DEH·zr·ee or DEH·zr·ay. It doesn't matter."

"Yes, it does. The correct pronunciation is DEH·zr·ay," she told me, "But it's your name so you should choose one and stick with it."

I want to be right, I thought. *Plus*, ray *at the end makes me think of the sun.*

"I'll go with DEH·zr·ay." From then on, I wasn't too shy to say my name, the right one, for I liked the sound of it.

I learned that Desiree meant "much desired" or "longed for." But was I? After all, some still called me "Desi" for short or poked fun at me with "Dizzy." And in sports I was picked last for teams.

When I hit my tweens, I began to like boys. I let them kiss me in the dark. All my friends paired up with beaus, but none of the boys chose me for their own. The name Desiree didn't seem to fit.

As for my second name, *Anne*, my mother passed it down from her own name, Nancy Anne. Later I passed it down to my daughter. I learned that Anne means "favored." But was I?

The family name, St. Clair, got its start in France, where Clair means "clear." I liked St. Clair, for it made my full name flow.

In high school, teachers saw my worth and pushed me to join clubs. In a race for a club seat, I used St. Clair in my play-on-words quip, "Vote for me! I'm a saint, not a sinner!" But was I? I thought of those deeds done in the dark.

After college I met a man who seemed to be my match. When he asked me to marry him, I thought about my soon-to-be new name, Desiree Glass. It fell flat when I spoke it out loud. I couldn't bear to give up St. Clair, so I dropped Anne and put St. Clair in its place.

It wasn't long until I found out that my new husband longed for strong drink more than he longed for me. In time, we broke up, and once again I thought about my name. Should I change it back to my given name? For the sake of my kids, I didn't. We would all still share Glass as our last name. But my first name truly didn't suit me now.

While my name stayed the same, my heart broke in two. The pain seemed more than I could bear. Yet I couldn't stay in a pit. I had kids to rear. Some way I found the strength to carry on. I worked hard to pay the bills and care for the needs of my family. But I had needs of my own. Would I ever feel whole? Ever live up to my name, Desiree?

I turned to my faith, went to church, and read the Bible. I reached out to friends and family. All of this gave me the boost to try new things, such as a new career as a teacher.

On the first day of school I said, "Hi, I'm Ms. Glass, Desiree

St. Clair Glass, and it is my desire to make things as clear as glass to you." I thought it was a good way for them to learn my name.

Many years have passed since I began my career. I don't doubt it was the right thing to do. It warms my heart each time I am able to cheer a child or point them in the way they should go.

Many years have also passed since I gave my heart to Jesus. He has fixed me up and freed me of my deeds done in the dark. I know who I am in Christ. *"I am my beloved's, and his desire is for me"* (Song of Solomon 7:10 NRSV). I am Desiree, "much desired."

I long to share this true love story with all those I meet. And while I can't say Jesus' name at school, I can bear His Light. I pray it shines from my face. May it be clear each time I greet a child.

When asked to work with a school girls club to help them find who they are and what they are called to do, of course I said yes. One day when our club met, a woman from our staff spoke on how to learn names. She said to see an image in your mind each time you think of the person. Then she turned to me and said, "For example, when I think of Ms. Glass, I see sun *rays* shining through a window."

Tears brimmed as I thought about what I had prayed — and also about the Lover of my soul, the One who tells me, "[Desiree], *I have redeemed you; I have called you by name, you are mine*" (Isa. 43:1 NRSV).

Yes, I am desired; I am favored. And that is as clear as glass.

17

Mary Frances

Mary Heitzman

Be sure to use both names!" Mom called as I ran out of our house for the first day of school.

I stopped. At age six I didn't want to say my full name of *Mary Frances*. Two names, each with two parts, were just too much.

Most kids I knew had names like Ann, Pat, Sue, Tom, or Mark. I didn't want the kids at school or the nuns or the priest to stare at me all the time I had to take up to say such a long name!

"I just want to say, Mary," I told Mom. "Not the whole thing." I felt as if a good stamp of my foot would add to my case, but that wasn't the way I was raised. So, I just asked, "Why?"

"You were named after both of your grandmas."

That much I knew. Mom's mom was named Mary. My Dad's mom was named Frances.

I also knew how much both my mom and my dad loved their mothers. And how they wished that my grandmas had lived to see me grow up, the first girl after three boys. All this even though my grandmothers had died when I was no more than a gleam in my mom's eyes.

As for eyes, my Dad would point out that my blue eyes were just like Grandma Theis'. And my mom told me how Grandma Grommesch would make her own mustard plasters to put on Mom's chest when she was sick, just like Mom did for me when I was sick.

I knew Mom was right about the name thing. And to please her, I learned to be brave. I said my full name on that first day of school and from then on. For a few months I had to force out "Mary Frances," but soon it made me feel good to honor both of my grandmas.

Time has changed the way I honor them, as I am now known by some friends as Mary and by others as Fran. And I'm so glad that my mom and dad told me stories about each of their moms and that they made it clear to me at the start of first grade to say both of their names.

To this day, I wish I had known those young mothers who broke ground to plant seeds that grew to food to feed their loved ones, who cooked on wood stoves to fill their homes with the smell of fresh-baked bread six days a week, while at the same time one raised eight kids and the other nine.

Even though I never met these grandmothers of mine, I hold them in my heart — proud of the way that my mom and dad held them in theirs.

18

I Am Ree

Shelley Pierce

I grew up in a family of five kids. Four girls and, the last, a boy.
My middle name is *Ree*.

Odd, you say? Yes.

Why, you ask? To rhyme with my sister, Dodie's middle name of *Lee*, of course.

I don't know if my mom and dad planned this middle-name-rhyme thing or if the names just fell into place.

None of my friends had the name Ree. I heard Ray, Ret, and Rod. There was even a Rex and a Rue.

Ree? None.

You must know, my mom did not stop with two rhymes.

Four girls in the family. And the middle names? Lee, Ree, Dee, and Marie.

I can read your mind. You want to know my brother's middle name. He has two.

Gary and Harold.

Since he was named after our dad and grandfather, his name didn't have to rhyme.

I didn't mind that I was the only Ree. I didn't need to fit in with friends at school. I fit in with my sisters. Rain or shine, sibling fights or peace, we fit like the best puzzle ever.

At the age of fifteen, I met my husband-to-be. We had long talks and, as we got to know each other, I learned his mother's middle name: *Rhea* (pronounced Ree). Years later, my last name changed to his — Pierce — and I knew.

This was meant to be. To say my name-twin was dear to me does not begin to tell the tale of our bond. She showed me Jesus. She taught me how to be the wife of the pastor. She taught me well, though she did not know that I watched. She did not know that I listened.

My sense of the best puzzle ever changed a bit. It was made whole only once I'd found . . . the other Ree (Rhea).

19

That's Not My Real Name

Patty Barry

The first time I thought much about names at all was when I was six years old and looked out our front door to see the strange man who had rung the bell.

"Is Colleen home?" he asked me.

"There is no Colleen here," I said and tried to shut the door.

But my dad heard me and laughed. "*Colleen*," he said, "is your mom's name! Of course she is home."

The man frowned at me and gave my mom a fresh peach pie from his wife, while I stood there in shock and thought about the odd fact that my mom had a name. *What?* I thought. *How can she be so much like us kids? Not just Mom, but also her own self? Colleen. Who would have thought such a thing?*

From that day on, I knew that we all have our own names, so when I went to first grade and the class had five girls with the same given name as mine, it made sense to us girls that each of us should have her own unique name at school. We met with Miss Clark and in no time, the five Patricia's names were said to be Patty, Patsy, Trisha, Patty Jo, and Pat. The name I liked least was Pat, but I was too shy to speak up, while none of them were, so soon the first four names were gone and all that was left for me was plain old *Pat*.

I went home that day and cried while I told my mom that now she had to call me Pat. Never again could she call me Patty.

No more could Aunt Nell call me Patsy Lee. No more was I me, Patty. And I asked her if God would still know me when I prayed, if I had to use a new name to ask for His help? Would He still help plain old Pat the way he used to look out for me when I was Patty? She said she was sure that He would.

In time, I got used to the name, though I never liked it. That I could change it, if I chose to, did not dawn on me. I was glad that my sweet mom still called me Patty and my great aunt still called me Patsy Lee, and God did still keep me safe — so I thought He must know me still, in spite of what I was called. But out in the world of school and with my friends, I was Pat and that was that.

When I got big and had a job, I told them I was Pat, and Pat was what my own kids were told was their mom's name. When I thought of it, I still felt sad, but I did not say that out loud. I thought it was too late, and it felt weird to change my name. Besides, as long as she lived, my mom still called me Patty; and I loved that.

But when my mom died, it felt as if I'd lost my real name for good, and one day I told that to some of my friends. They laughed. "Fine!" they said. "From now on we will call you by your real name, Patty." And they did! In a short time, I once more thought of Me by the name I liked best, and most of those in my life thought of me by that name as well.

Yes, I got my name back, but I have to say that in time I was just as glad to get some new names too — like Grandma and Mimi. In fact, it was good for a laugh when my friend came by and saw me with my small grandson. She called out, "Hi, Patty! And who is that cute young man with you there?" I had no time to speak when a wee voice piped up with, "There is no Patty here. This is my Mimi, and I am Mac."

Boy was he in for a shock to learn that I had a name!

I knew just how he felt.

20

A Wee Orph

Frank Caudle

Each of us has a name. It is ours by the choice of our moms or dads. We had no say in it.

They made the pick, and we must live with it. All we have is the choice to be glad or sad about it. Or we can change it. But the legal way costs big bucks.

My father was set on what name I would wear. He gave me all three of his. I was to be called by name number two. No one could change it.

My middle name is *Orpheus*.

In grade two or three my life of jokes began.

For you Greek nerds and to set the course straight for the rest, Orpheus was well known for his music and art and also as a poet — skills I do not have. So the gift of that name was of no use good to me.

All through my young years, I was called "Orph." With a name like that, how did I make it to be an adult? At first, I did not take the jests well. But over time, I began to just go the flow. I knew that if I did not let it rile me, the jokes would soon pass. That was a hard thing for me to learn. But, once I did, life in school took a turn for the best, and I had gained a skill to use later in times of stress.

But the name Orph went on to when I was grown up. Even while still in the womb, our first baby was called "little Orph."

At one point, though, my wife said, whoa! If we were to have a boy, he would not be the third. No more Orpheus. Well, our son is glad we did not pass the name on so he did not have puns thrown at him all the time.

I leave you with this: If you are about to pick a name for your child, first think long and hard. You are in the now, but he will have to live with your choice for the rest of his life. So for his sake, you will want to shy away from names like Orpheus.

21

What's Your Name?

Doris Hoover

How can one small name be so hard to say? *Barndt.* Go on, try it. I bet you said it wrong. In fact, I'm sure you said it wrong. With one vowel, and the word *barn* in it, you'd think it would be a cinch next to names like Tomaszewski or Czyzewich. But, no, it's a name that tricks the eye.

Since I grew up with that last name, I had to get used to all the ways that it could be said. When asked my name, I'd say it, then spell it. I even gave hints like "It's barn with a *d-t.*" But that didn't help. Blank stares meant I had to say it and spell it more than once. I would tell them, "To pronounce my name, simply skip the *d* and say Barnt. It rhymes with aren't."

So where did my strange name come from? I checked files and learned it may have been spelled wrong on Ellis Island. My guess is the man with the pen mixed up the *r* and the *a* and wrote Barndt when it should have been Brandt, which is how most say my name. Or it may have come from the name Berndt.

When I got married, I thought my life would change. I mean, how hard can Hoover be? But no, my fate goes on. People hear Hooper or Huber. Or they spell it "H-o-v-e-r."

So when asked, I say "Hoover like the vacuum," but that clicks only with old folks. If I say, "Hoover with a *v*," they hear *b*, *d*, *p*, or *t* instead of *v*. Most of the time I just do what I used to do — say it and then spell it. Now, when I'm asked my name, I say, "Hoover, with a *v* — for Victory!"

22

Elizabeth Ann

Liz Kimmel

My given, name, *Elizabeth*, is both regal and quaint. Some well-known Elizabeths have gone ahead of me, such as two queens of England, a multi-wed star of the screen and stage, and John the Baptist's mom from the Bible. While the world at large does not know me as they do these other Elizabeths, I am thrilled to share this most basic label with them — our name.

I came into this world as a tiny baby, less than five pounds. My brothers called me "Little-Bit." Some of them still do to this day, though I am not so tiny any more. As I grew, my family called me "Liz." That was okay, I guess. But my sister had a friend (also an Elizabeth), who went by Betsy. How I wished I had been named Betsy. It was a grand name, a name not heard as often as the very plain Liz. My young heart was filled with envy. But I didn't want that envy to alter who I was, and since no one would refer to me as Betsy, I gave in to the crowd and let them call me what they would.

I once asked my dad why they chose the name they did for me. My older brothers are John, David, and Bruce — run-of-the-mill names, not fancy. My sister is Mari. She is the only Mari I knew for many years, which means her name is rare. Lucky duck! So why Elizabeth? Not rare. Not fancy. Run-of-the-mill. He had no answer for me. I don't know if they chose my name ahead of time or not. After my mom passed away in the course of my birth, did he have to choose all alone? Maybe a nurse named

Elizabeth helped him through this awful time. Maybe he saw it in a book or had a close friend by that name. Maybe he and Mom did talk about it and planned my name. I often wished I'd found out why. But I never did.

And then, why Liz? I could have been Beth . . . Libby . . . Ellie . . . Eliza . . . Lily . . . Etta . . . Betsy. Would any of these have made my heart glad? We'll never know. I did love Beth as a top choice, so much that we named our daughter Bethany. (I sure didn't want an Elizabeth Junior.) Over the years she has been Beth, Bethy, and Buffy (when her older brother couldn't say the *th* sound very well), and now her husband calls her just *B*. It's nice to have so many names to pick from.

In later years I came to love my name. When I learned what it meant — gift of God or oath of God — I was glad of the choice that my dad made at my birth. As a young girl, I thought I was to blame for my mom's death. I tried to please Dad so he would love me and not be mad at me. But God soothed my angst. He taught my heart to trust in His oath, His vow, His word over my life. *"I know the plans I have for you,"* He tells me, *"plans to prosper you and not to harm you, plans to give you hope and a future"* (Jeremiah 29:11 NIV). To know that I was a gift from God to my dad, even in the loss of his wife, made me want to love both even more.

One of my brothers chose an Elizabeth Ann to be his wife. So for a while there were two of us with the exact same name (first, middle, and last), who were the same age (only four months apart), and housed in the same abode. When a shout would ring through the house for a Liz, we both chimed in. If the phone rang and they asked for Liz, we both jumped up. In order to tell who was who, she got to be Liz, and I came to be Lizzy. What!? They couldn't call me Betsy? Oh, well. A few years later, after I wed Cary, that changed. Once I moved out of the group house and into our new home, I went back to being Liz. A sweet gift from God to Cary was a wife named Elizabeth, as that had been the girl's name he loved the best ever since he was a young boy.

Cool side-bar — Bruce and his Liz had four girls, and here is proof that they loved our name so much. Each of the girls has Elizabeth as her middle name.

The *Ann* part of my name means as much to me as Elizabeth does. It means *grace* or *favor*. God's grace showed up right away in the form of my Angel Moms (three moms who shared me over the course of my life and loved me with all of their hearts). Many times God's hand of grace has turned me from a wrong path. I've heard Him speak to my heart and give me words to say and words to write. His grace has watched over every step I take.

My husband often points out the favor I have. Most often it's when we need to ask for some kind of help at the bank or with an order on Amazon or an item we can't find or many other types of needs. I get to be the one who makes the phone calls for info, for in Cary's eyes, "They just get mad at me, but they seem to want to help you." That's the favor part. At times I wish Cary would just make the calls, but that's where grace steps in again.

God's gift, God's vow, God's grace, God's favor. I'll keep them all! I am full of thanks for the name given to me after such a hard event and with no plan on the part of my dad. God knew my name. God calls me by my name. And I want to reply to that call with an eager "Yes!"

23

A Girl of Many Names

Martha Rogers

"Mar-tha! Da-vid! Come to sup-per!" My mom would stress the last part of each word and also raise her voice high. Mom was a great cook, so my brother and I would rush home from points far and wide where we would climb trees, ride bikes, and play with small chicks on our farm.

As the years passed, I gained my fair share of nicknames. It started at Girl Scout camps where my friends would tease me and call me "Chicken," or "Stick-in-the-Mud," or "Miss Prissy." Even worse were the many jokes and tricks that my good-girl ways would bring my way. Just to get a rise out of me, they'd string my clothes up the flagpole. They said they pulled those pranks because they loved me. I said, "God save me from that kind of love!"

Since I would fret about most things and most of the time, I got called "worry wart" a lot. My glasses and braces earned me the names "four eyes" and "metal mouth."

I don't want to go back to those days again.

Even though I was also known as "sweet Martha," my real goal was to look good and be well liked. Oh to be one of the cool kids!

It took a while for me to grow out of that. College days held ups and downs. I was still sweet Martha and loved to sing. The label I earned after graduation was "elementary school music teacher." Those were the days! With a song in my heart, I taught those kids to sing and have fun.

After I tied the knot with my Navy pilot husband, medical school in Maine was in the cards for us. As a new wife, I had to go to work to pay the bills while Doug was in school. We were as poor as church mice, but those days brought such joy. I found my way to the stage and played roles such as Grace in *Annie*, Marion in *The Music Man*, Yum Yum in *The Mikado*, and Josephine in *HMS Pinafore*. What a thrill! Those were names I loved to be called, since with each I got to act the part.

These days, my best-loved name is Mom which I won when two small China dolls found their way into our hearts. From dress up to make up, our girls grew up fast.

Since our friends saw me as a woman armed with grit, guts, and grace, they would call me Mary Poppins and "Fancy Martha."

The good girl in me stayed, and I did love nice clothes and nice things. I did not think a girl with those apt names would end up on a farm with three horses, three dogs, and three cats. But I did. Because I was still Miss Prissy and Fancy Martha, we made it a joke to call our farm Green Acres. The name stuck.

The short and sweet of it is that of all my names — from Stick-in-the-Mud to Mary Poppins — I have come to love one name most of all: Child of God. My identity is found in Him, and my last stop is heaven.

I have been able to ***taste and see that the Lord is good*** (Psalm 34:8 NIV) and learn that He loves each of us just the way we are. Since ***there is no other name under heaven given to mankind by which we must be saved*** (Acts 4: 12, NIV), each of us can find our all in all in Him.

24

By Any Other Name

Wilma Vernich

When I was a young girl, my name didn't give me a sense of pride. Back then, *Wilma* was my name, and shame was my game.

Now I think, *How sad. What a waste of time for me to fret over what kids said about my name!*

A child can get teased for so many things. In my case, kids had lots of food for the fodder whether it was my hair, my weight, my feet, my home-sewn clothes, my religion, or my name. It was hard for me to be a Wilma in a world of cute names like Lori, Tammy, Cindy, Lisa, Becky, Debbie, Dana, Toni, and Wendy. Oh, how I longed to be a Wendy! Could I just keep the *W* and scratch over the *i-l-m-a* to add *e-n-d-y*? Just for a day, I would have loved to be a plain Jane with a name like Wendy Smith.

All Fred and Wilma Flintstone jokes aside:

"I have a pig named Wilma," The rude kid in my sixth-grade class laughed.

"I've never heard of a name like that. Did you say 'William'?" (Duh — do I look like a boy?)

"You *look* like your name." I would have liked to think the mean girl meant it for good, but I didn't take it that way.

Thanks to my middle-school English teacher, the tide began to turn for me in eighth grade. When she found out my middle name was *Rose*, in front of the whole class she said, "Wilma Rose

— what a *beautiful* name for a beautiful girl!" Bless her heart; she must have seen how much I yearned to hear those words. My blush turned my cheeks pink and from then and through the rest of the year, my peers called me "Rosie." I loved it!

When the guy I was dating in college (now my husband) went home for spring break and told his best friend he liked a girl named Wilma, his friend quipped, "Her name is Wilma, huh? Sounds to me like you're dating somebody's grandma!"

At least I was well known in college since no one else in the whole college bore my name. My good friends — and some really cute guys — would yell clear across campus at me, like Fred Flintstone did to his red-haired wife: "WIL-MAAAAA!"

Though the road to get there took some time, I am glad to say that since those days, I have grown into my old-lady name. I've learned to laugh, lean into, and love it. After all, as Robert Frost said, "The only way out is through."

Old names are all the rage now — names like Emma, Hazel, Alice, Ava, Olivia, Beatrice, Walter, Harry, George, Elijah, Jonah, and the like. I read a list not too long ago titled "40 Baby Names from the Past" that are making a run with new moms and dads. My sister's name, Dorothy, made the list at the eleventh spot and Betty, my Flintstone sidekick, ranks as fourteen on the list.

Shirley, at this rate the name Wilma will break the top one hundred list soon.

At least, I'll hold out hope for — WIL-MAAAAA!

25

What My Name Isn't

Candice Weathers

I'm from the South, where every wrong way to say or spell names is just a part of life. Most of the time it is not meant to be mean. That isn't the way it's done here. We are very subtle — until we're not.

There comes a time, though, when enough is enough. At age forty-eight, I have lived on this earth for almost half a century and the time has come for people to listen up! By dint of age alone, I have earned the right for my name to be my name, for people to get it right!

It's not hard. My name is *Candice*. I use it in print all the time — on paper, on checks and on nice return-address labels. It's how I sign both my home and work email – Candice. It's not spelled Candace or Candis or Candus. When in doubt, all one has to do is copy and paste my name from where it sits — in bold sixteen-point font at the bottom half of the screen.

Note to my aunts and uncles and cousins: I've been blessed to know you all for decades so you should know that my name is not Candance. Nor is it Candense (ha ha). I know you had to think about it when you wrote my name on my fortieth birthday cards. The ink globs in the middle where you wrote it wrong were a dead giveaway! No – this is not a dig that I don't get cards anymore, Aunt Julia. This is a real thing that you all need to fix.

I used to have a nickname, "Candy." That name has been

said and spelled wrong as well — like Cindy, Candie, Cadie. Can someone tell me how anyone can get it that wrong? What five-year-old can't spell candy when they write their list to Santa Claus? I bet you who spell that name wrong have a bag of sweets in your house right now that you can use to spellcheck. If that fails, you can just watch TV for the M&M commercials, for Pete's sake!

You know who gets it right? Third grade kids. Even when the teacher got it wrong and wrote my full name on my cubby as Candy Pee (not Lee) Linkous, third grade kids got the name right — all year long. They got it right all the way into fourth and fifth grades, too. Of course, bless your heart, Arvis, you still knew the right way to spell it when we were twenty-five and as a joke you called me "Candy Pee" in the line at Kroger's. You got two gold stars my friend, while I smiled my sweet smile that means *I will get you when you go to sleep.*

I had high hopes when I got older and my name changed to Candice. My optimism started in my youth. Candice is a grown-up name, a woman's name. Then my hopes died when I saw what should have been my name on the high-school billboard when I made the Honor Roll: Candic Likous. Yes, Mr. Farley, I know the *e* just fell off, but what about the letter you left out of my last name? That trauma took a few years to get past. I still have to work on it a bit from time to time.

I know, I know. It's just a name! Yet I find that I like me – and my name – more and more the older and more mature I get. Names have a kind of power; it's the first thing we are taught about ourselves that lasts for our whole life.

Of course, it is also just good manners to speak and spell a name right. I do try to be nice, as I was raised to be. In fact, with this twang of mine (which I've been told is as sweet and smooth as the spring rain on a rose in bloom) some sounds can be a little too soft. But note to work-buddy Ray: If I can say your jacked up last name and spell it right every time, you can learn that my name is not Kansas! I don't care what else you need to put in your morning coffee, add that my name is not a state!

Well, there you go. I've said my piece. One great thing about going through life with a name like mine? You learn to stand up for yourself and make people take note, one way or the other — even if they still may miss the spelling on a word that's been around since A.D. 1000.

How many can say that about their name?

26

Hurricane Bob

Jeanne Roberson

When Bob and I wed on September 1, 1991, pink and white beach roses with purple astors adorned the beds on both sides of the deck at the Viking Hotel in Newport, Rhode Island. Blue skies with a light sea breeze made it a nice day to wed. Our loved ones sat close by under a white tent as we gazed deep into each other's eyes and said our vows. Soon after the ballroom doors were open, the aroma of a Steamship Round Roast* filled the air.

At one point we weren't sure that the wedding was even going to come off — what with downed trees and closed roads. The Newport bridge we had to cross was closed as well.

Category Two Hurricane Bob had hit Newport a week prior to our wedding date.

"Do you think this is a sign?" my friends joked. "Are you sure you want to so do this?" they laughed.

It's just a funny coincidence, I thought.

Bob and I went on to have two daughters and lived in a small town on the east coast of Rhode Island. The first few years were filled with bliss, but it wasn't to last. Sad to say, the time came for us to part ways.

I moved to Florida with my two girls to make a fresh start and mend my heart.

For his part, Bob met a woman with three daughters. They married and all moved into the same house we had lived in. This might not have been an issue had she not had the same name as me. She even spelled it the same way, *Jeanne*.

From a legal stand point, it caused a bit of chaos.

Bob and I kept a court-ordered bank account for child support at the same bank where he and his new wife had a joint account. Once in a while the bank tellers asked if I had more than one account. A special password password had to be added to my account, and I soon had to change banks.

To add to the upset, from time to time we received each other's mail. (I loved some of her magazines.) At one point, I was buying a home in Florida when the bank processing my loan found an error. My credit report and hers had been merged. Someone had seen the same name and address but failed to see that the social security numbers and birth dates weren't the same.

As if it wasn't enough to lose the love of my life, who could have dreamed he would marry a woman with the same name as mine and give her the same address?

It was a mess, to say the least. Still at times I just had to laugh.

Be that as it may, life has twists and turns. Three years into their marriage Jeanne and her children left Bob alone and sad.

Guess who was the first one he called?

At one time I might have been glad for his pain and loss so he'd know how it felt to be the one who was left alone. But my Christian heart wouldn't let me. I didn't feel any joy in his pain. In fact, I felt sad for him, for her children, and for mine. With open arms I wrapped him in love.

Over the next few years, we split holidays and free time between Florida and Rhode Island. It was a long, hard road back, but on September 1 (our original wedding day), in 2015, we once again walked down the aisle — this time in a small Baptist church on Block Island. We didn't tell a soul, not even our children, until we came back. We said our vows in front of God, a pastor, and two strangers we'd met at our hotel who stood up with us.

Since then, we've seen our first daughter marry and our youngest graduate from college. We are now proud grandparents. Life is not easy, but we work through the tough times, forgive each other, and move on.

Jeanne took back her own last name and moved to her home state. Her daughters are grown and she is a grandmother now, too. These days, I have only good thoughts for her and wish her rosy health and much joy in her life.

Bob was a hurricane that came ashore to land in my life. But today I bathe in the calm after the storm.

* A Steamship Round of beef is roast that consists of the whole round with the rump and heel. It's easy to carve and popular at formal buffets and weddings.

27

The Namesake

Gene C. Burgess

What's in a name? In mine, the *C* stands for a man named Charles Augustus Hicks, my grandfather. He drank a lot of booze his whole life. When my mom was small, fear of Charles and the booze kept her out of the house most of the time. I can "see" him in his old chair, his Army hat by his side. He never said much to me. I am glad I carry his name. Why? I am not sure. But with his name, I gain a link to the past, and I care for him since his life was one source of my life.

For over forty years, Franklin, one of my old pals, has called me *C*, just C. He had never heard of Charles Augustus Hicks, but began to call me C when he could not speak after he broke his neck in a motorcycle crash. He could only say a few words and C must have been easy for him. The sound of Franklin's C stirs a deep cord in my soul. It brings a tear to my eye for C said in just that way can come only from Franklin. He is an 'ole friend, and you can't make 'ole friends. I would not allow a new friend to call me C. That right is set aside for Franklin, as it is his sign of love for me.

But what else is in *my* name?

My friend Robert Waltman found "Bene Gurgess," in that name. He called me that all the time. When he did, his face wore a big smile. He thought it funny to switch the first letters of my name. I, in turn, found humor in Waltman.

Ben Hines found his own twist on Gene. I may like Ben all the time, but when he calls me "Geno," I love him. When he says Geno he smiles big, and I know my name brings him joy. Or is there joy in Ben all the time?

Then there is Eric McIntyre. He is a mason who works with me. Every time he calls me "Mr. B." it fills me with joy. I see the honor on his face, which in turn, brings to my mind that a few of my dad's friends called him Mr. B. Eric reminds me to honor my dad. Does my name bring honor on its own, or is Eric full of honor when he calls me Mr. B?

My young friend Bethany calls me "Mr. Gene." She says my name with a calm pause first, as if she is vague about what to call me. Is he boss? Friend? In no other place in my life do I hear that calm. Could it be that a sense of calm flows from Bethany?

Mom had a way with my name. When she said, "Gene Charles," I knew I was in trouble. She could call my name today, from heaven, and I would know who it was. Were I to hear Gene with Charles, I would know that she, Dad — or maybe even God — was on the hunt for me. And it would not be good.

My last name, *Burgess*, hides some gems. I tell people we are English and that Burgess comes from the House of Burgesses. If that is true or not, I do not know. But I do know this: I am pleased to be the son of Edsel and Donna Burgess. They were quiet people who never made much of a splash in the pond of life.

But when I would paint, my mom would sit up with me until 2:00 A.M. I loved to sell my work at her door. I came to her with my goods and every time, she would buy them. Inside of Burgess was a great Mom.

Also hidden in Burgess is a Dad who helped to bring me into being, although for him it was easy. Mom did all the hard work to get me here, but after that Dad did work hard to clothe and feed me and my six siblings. My parents taught me that honor, love, and grace live in the name Burgess. Or was it just that honor, love, and grace lived in them?

It is also things you put with a name that make it great. Nick, my nephew, calls me "Uncle Gene." I love it. It is so nice for him to voice how close we are when he adds uncle. Or is being nice just inside of Nick?

Two other names of this type are "Pastor Gene" (even though I am not a pastor) and "Brother Gene." These are what my friends at church call me. I see love in the ones who use those names. When Dwight, Steve, Dena, and more call me Pastor, I think they show what is in their hearts.

In the names on this list, I see human beings full of care, love, honor, joy, calm, and more. I see these life values in their hearts when I hear their names.

All of this is in our names — and so much more.

28

Thank You for Your Service

Terry Magness

"It's Terry with a *Y*. . . . No, it's two *R*s. . . . Just think of Terry and the Pirates. . . . You've never heard of Terry and the Pirates? Hmmm, I guess that was before your time."

Now I've done it. He knows how old I am. At least he hasn't asked me for the exact date of my birth — yet!

And so it goes. The other day I got mail to Mr. Terry Magness. Though this occurs often, I was caught by this one's legal look. It was hard to miss the words that spread across the top of the large brown pack from The American Legion Benefits Department: "Enacted by Congress" and "*URGENT* PLEASE RUSH" and "Thank you for your loyal service!" *For my service?* I have never been in the armed services — that is apart from my being a civilian G2 clerk/typist for an Army OCS Company next door to my husband's OCS Company. In any case, that was back in the dark ages.

I tore open one end and pulled out a Certificate of Honor for my military service. My jaw dropped, and to tell you the truth, it crossed my mind to keep it — just because I could. My husband, on the other hand, did not agree I should. So, to honor my veteran, I tossed it into file thirteen. My loss.

But not all is lost. While doing some research years ago, I learned that the name *Terry* comes from the name *Theresa*, which means "harvester." My family name, *Engel*, means "angel" in

German. So being the wordsmith that I am, I joined the two and came up with "harvesting angel." I like that, and considering the years I've served in missions and ministry, I find that name quite apt. With my name I will be content until the day when my Father gives me a new name that right now only He knows.

29

A Unique Name

Linda L. Kruschke

Before our first child was born, my husband and I picked names for both a boy and a girl since we didn't know which we would have.

If we had a son, we wanted his nickname to be "Ben." To make sure no one ever called him Benji, we ruled out Benjamin. We chose *Benton* because it was unique. It turned out to be a good call.

In his pre-school class, there were two Benjamins, a Bennett, and our son Benton. If we had named him Benjamin, odds are he would have been the Benji in the class. Instead, they called him by his full first name so one of the Benjamins could be called Ben. From then on, he was known as Benton. If anyone called him Ben he would say, "My name is Benton." And that was that.

For his middle name I wanted to use my maiden name. My husband agreed. "But can we spell it without the *W*?" he asked.

"No," I said, "that would defeat the whole point. I don't like the name enough to call him Benton Roland."

When I was single, it drove me nuts when people spelled my last name wrong. I would say my name and before I had a chance to spell it, they would write Roland — even if I stressed the *w* at the end of the first syllable. The right spelling is R-o-**w**-l-a-n-d. If our son's middle name was to be Rowland, it must be spelled right.

On the whole, he has a good and apt name that fits his

personality quite well. Still, we've found it hard to find souvenirs with his name when we go on vacation. We found key rings and license plates with Ben, Benjamin, Bennett, and even Benson, but never Benton. Unique has its price. But the price is worth it when you find custom gifts — such as the railroad spike stamped with his name by a blacksmith in Keystone, South Dakota. It cost us time and a few more bills than a key ring, but he still has it.

If your name is James or Robert or Fred, you don't think much about what famous or fictional people might have the same name. But when your name is Benton, you know each and every one. You know that on *The Adventures of Jonny Quest*, Jonny's dad is Dr. Benton Quest. You know that the son of country singer Suzy Bogguss is named Benton and was born the same day as you. Benton Fraser is a fictional Canadian Mountie on the early '90s TV show. You know that there aren't many more well-known Bentons.

Once when Benton was fifteen, we drove up north to see my sister and her family. Along the route we saw a huge sign that read "Dennis Benton for County Commissioner." Benton was in large letters and took up most of the sign.

"Ha," Benton said, "that guy has a first name for a last name."

"Umm, truth be told," I said, "you have a last name for a first name, and a last name for a middle name, and, well, a last name for a last name. You have no first name."

Benton had not ever thought of this. He was not thrilled by this news and did not think it was as funny as we did.

30

Little Angelia's Gonna Sing

A. DiAnne Wilson

Each week, the girl sang on the air waves.
My mom fell in love with her voice,
So when the time came to give me a name
Angelia was her top choice.

But Gran thought she should choose, too.
DiAnne is what I'd go by.
So they met mid-way and still to this day
I'm Mom's "Angel" and Gran's "Di."

31

The Name Game

Susan Cheeves King

Strike One in my name game was shared by all five of us in the family — the last name of *Cheeves*. Early on, we each had to learn to live with the wrong ways to say it — CHEH-vees, Cheever, Chives, CHEE-vehss — even Chavez (when the right way rhymes with *leaves*). And we all know how much guys love nicknames. So my brother was called "Cheesy," "Cheeseburger," and "Larry Cheeves with bologna on top."

When I wed, I was glad to trade up. *King* is a great name; it even has a ring to it! And at last — a name no one ever would ask me to spell. Wrong! Strike Two! Early on, I found that a caller could hear Keene or Kane instead of King. After this occurred a few times, I began to just rattle off, "Susan King — K-I-N-G" and have done so on every phone call since.

What's more, it wasn't too long until I felt the full sense that I had given up a unique name for one shared by every Tom, Dick, and Harry. I began to miss times with Cheeves that King could never bring me. One was when I worked at J.C. Penney during high school and a man with less charm than he thought he had asked me, "Are you really that mischievous?" When I looked perplexed, he pointed to my badge and said, "Aren't you Miss Cheeves-ious?"

And with what other name could a church that had just hired my dad to preach greet us on our welcome potluck with their take on an old hymn, "Bringing in the Cheeves"?

Over the years, I did find fun in the King name as well. My husband, Joe, first chose to revel in the full sense of his name with a customized California license plate: JOKING.* One day we were driving around our hometown of Palm Springs in our pale-blue Ford Pinto and pulled up behind a car with the same make, model, and year as ours — even the same color. What fun to also find out how close that car's plate was to ours since it read "HA HA"! Don't you know that we just had to honk to catch their eye and then — with only a look to seal the deal — we and the other car tooled around town side by side to enjoy the looks on the faces of everyone who also got the joke.

Our kids — starting with our first — loved their last name. Once, I found out that one of my best students lived in the same dorm, and on the same floor, as my son. "Oh," I said, "you must know my son, James King?" After he said no, I was ready to move on. But then, his face lit up as he said, "Oh — King James!" (Every afternoon in kindergarten, James loved to come home from school and read the King James Version of the Bible.) Later, our second son became "King David" to his friends. Even our daughter joined in — but only as far as her choice of "kingjenn" to start her email address (which she kept long after she wed).

Years later, our grandkids got in on the fun. When for the hundredth time I felt I had to remind our four-year-old grandson David, "You know Grandpa wasn't being serious," I loved his reply: "He can't be any other way, Grandma. He's always Joking."

These days, when we meet someone new, I tell them that they will have an easy time with our names — at least Joe's, that is — adding, "The only thing he's serious about is his name — Joe King."

Before I was born, my parents knew what two other names they were going to give me — just not their order. They chose *Lynette* and *Susan*. One came from my father, Lyndell. This name

75

was to come first if I seemed to be a quiet, low-key baby. If not, they would call me "Susie." By the time I was a day old, Susie had claimed the first-name spot.

Of course my legal name is Susan — which they chose because they had never known anyone by that name. Sad-to-say, it seems that half the country must have thought the same thing as it was in fifth place for girl's names that birth year. In the second grade, I was one of seven Susans. (I had to be "Susie C.") In fourth grade, when we were taught Spanish and told to choose a Spanish first name, only the Susans had to pick names other than their own (once the teacher had given Susannah to her class pet, that is.)

Susie held sway until I ran into my eighth-grade history teacher, Mr. Slovik. The first time I heard him call the roll in his thick Boston accent — "Mahruhlyn, Baabrwa, Syoozie" — I felt like a stripper or fan dancer. The next class meeting, I told him my name was Susan, and I kept the name in school and my career from that point on.

That's when I learned that some people will just call you what they will. Ann, a new friend that year, made a point to tell me that she'd like to call me a name that no one else ever used. We settled on Sue. But the school day after she played at my house for the first time, she ran up to me with the words, "You are the biggest liar!" Shocked, I stood there while she claimed, "Your brother and sister call you Sue!" And I stayed shocked even after she said this. I'd never really thought about what they called me, that to each other we weren't Susie, Larry, and Donna but Su, Lar, and Don. Once calm again, Ann came up with her own name for me — that I swore would be one-of-a-kind in my list of names: "Susie-Q."

A few decades ago, a new name came my way. Jim — who shared twenty-one years with me at *The Upper Room* magazine — calls me "Suze." I like it. Its sound flies in the face of how I fear

I'm seen at times. (My daughter's phone ringtone for me hints at this — the theme from *Law and Order*.)

I've begun to miss being Susie to folks. Don't get me wrong; I don't want to go back to that old stage name from my devil-may-care pole-dance years. (In other words, I will keep Susan as my professional name.) I just wish that all the close friends I've made since eighth grade — most of whom call me Susan — would switch to the name of my youth. I know it's hard. Thirty years ago, a good friend tried but failed to make the change. I haven't asked since. But two friends have asked me if they could use the name they've heard family call me. And when they do, I feel as if I have flown back in time to my much-loved childhood.

*When we bought a second car, Joe just had to lobby for that car to sport a personalized plate as well, but I soon rejected his choice: SULKING. And that's when I knocked the ball out of the park!

32

Seventh Time's the Charm

Penny Hunt

No joke. My name has changed seven times. And I've been able to pull this off with no jail time.

Here's the list:

Pamela Lynn Scudder:	On the day I was born, in *The Virginia Gazette*, Williamsburg, Virginia.
Penny Lynn Scudder:	On my birth papers (Mom liked Penny more than Pamela.)
Penny Lynn Makoske:	When Frank R. Makoske gave both of us his name.
Penelope Lynn Makoske:	Not my name. Never has been. But when Sister Mary Paracleta said it was — it was!
Cecelia Makoske:	My saint's name for Catholic Confirmation.
Mrs. Glen J. Rehm:	My married name for a short time.
Mrs. William B. Hunt:	My married name for the past forty-three years.
Señora Penelope de Hunt:	My must-have name in South America.

Each name change has a tale to tell. Some tales are good and some not so good, but for the most part, *Penny* has been a life-long source of angst for me.

When "Penelope" was put on the board in third grade, the kids thought it had the same look to it as the fruit, cantaloupe, so it was turned into a tease in rhyme. What fun!

In fifth or sixth grade, Penny became "One cent, one cent, nothing but a one cent." A name of no worth that made me feel the same. Until — ta-da! — my grandfather told me I was, "One sent from heaven," and his special angel. God bless you, Grandpa.

And God bless Homer for *The Iliad* and *the Odyssey*. At long last, Penelope was a cool name to have! In case you don't know, she's the star of the tale and my hero. I chose not to fight to be called Penny instead of Penelope this time. I was proud of the name and glad to own it.

It took a day in court to change Rehm back to Makoske. A sad day and not a good time at all.

But it was the best day of my life when I took Mrs. William B. Hunt as my name, and it has been my name ever since. But one name glitch was still to come.

When Bill was picked as the American Naval Attaché in Ecuador, South America, I went to training for the wives of attachés at the Defense Intelligence Agency in Washington, D.C.

Near the end of the training, one of the other wives, from a South American country, took me to one side and said, "My mother says I must talk to you."

"About what?" I said.

"Your name."

"My name?"

"Yes. You cannot be Penny in South America. You must be Penelope."

"What do you mean? Why can't I be Penny?"

"You do not want to be called Penny for the same reason Richard would not want to be called Dick."

It took some time for me to get that, and when I did, we both grew red in the face.

So, for a time, I was Señora Penelope de Hunt. I grin each time that name shows up in the odd piece of mail.

That was a bit of a shock, but not as big a shock as the day I learned my name is etched in stone and sits at the site of a grave. A few years prior to my birth, Penny Lynn Scudder was born to my parents and died just two weeks later. My mother gave me her name.

When I asked, "Why? Why did you do that, Mom? Why didn't you give me a name of my own?"

"Because," she said, "I always wanted a Penny. My father told me, 'as long as you have a penny, the devil can never tempt you.'"

All I could do was blink. And then I did what I've found is best to do at times like that: let it go, and move on.

One day the other Penny and I will both have new names of our own. Our names will be etched on new white stones given to us by God. *"He who has an ear, let him hear what the Spirit says to the churches. To him who overcomes I will give . . . him a white stone, and on the stone a new name written which no one knows except him who receives it"* (Revelation 2:17 NKJV).

Until then, yours truly,

Pamela Penny Scudder Penelope Cecilia Makoske Rehm Hunt, a.k.a ???

33

Where Have You Gone, Joe DiMaggio?

Diana DiMaggio

My grandfather grew up in Sicily with his first cousin, "the Yankee Clipper" Joe DiMaggio. In my youth, his was a household name, and I was proud to be his kin. Now, Joe's fifty-six game hitting streak still stands eighty years later. But Joe DiMaggio was loved not just for his hitting stats, but for his traits of honor and humility. Such traits seem rare in today's sports heroes, as made note of in the Simon & Garfunkel song "Mrs. Robinson" from *The Graduate:* "Where have you gone, Joe DiMaggio? Our nation turns its lonely eyes to you"?

Joe DiMaggio was also a romantic hero, well known and loved for his zeal to care for one of Hollywood's most famous stars, Marilyn Monroe — even after their divorce. After her tragic death in August 1962, Joe showed the world what "until death do us part" means on a soul level. For the next twenty years, he sent six fresh red roses to her grave three times a week. He quit only when it began to cause too much public drama.

Of course, I could not live up to his fame or even my brother Pete's small-scale baseball-all-star rank. Nope! You will never find me in a place where a hard ball — or even a soft one — can hurl at my face, and I have only a bat to fend it off!

But could I ever swim! One year my coach, Jill, chose to enter me in the backstroke at our Hawaii State Championship. On the day of the meet, I gave in to my fear of a last-place finish and asked her to let me scratch the event, but she wouldn't. So, like any smart eleven-year-old girl, I hid under the far-off stands so I could say that I had not heard the event's call. But when Jill sent the whole team to look for me, I was found in time. To call her words a "scold" would be too kind. After that, I made a beeline to my lane and dove into the pool.

Sure that no one — not the swimmers in the lanes next to me, nor my Timer — could tell tears from just a wet face, I took a firm grip of the starting bar. As I hung in wait for the gun to sound, the Timer bent down and spoke in my ear, "It's okay, DiMaggio. Any friend of Marilyn's is a friend of mine." I laughed for most of the first twenty-five meters and still wonder today if that bronze medal could have been a gold had I just been more like my famed relative and put more trust in my coach — and myself.

34

Jud the Jud I

Judson I. Stone

What's in a name? Jokes, heritage, and later — thanks.

When I was a boy I did not like my first name. It was not Jack, Bob, Bill, Dave, or Steve. My name was *Judson*. I did like my last name — *Stone* — since it was nice and hard.

When I was young, my clan gave me nicknames, like "Juddy-pu." They joked and tried to bug me when they called me this girly name. They called me Juddy-pu because it was cute to them. That's what a nickname is for, isn't it, to tease or to sound cute.

My full name is Judson Irwin Stone. The Stones have lived a long time in the new world. My kin sailed in 1635 and lived in Watertown, Massachusetts. I am proud of that, but I did not have a part in it. They came three-hundred-twenty years before I was born. My first name comes from my mother's clan. My great-grandfather Judson Kilbourn was a surgeon in Utica, New York.

My mother's brother was Uncle Judson. I looked up to him because he was tall and looked huge to a young boy. I liked that he named his son Judson, but it still did not make me like my name.

Uncle Irwin, my father's brother, was a doctor. I liked him, but I did not like his name. To me, it had a strange sound. When we went to his house in Watertown, New York, he paid my brothers and me to weed his lawn. We earned one cent for each weed we picked. Boy, were we rich! "Can we pick more?" we would ask him.

My names have a rich heritage, but only after I took Christ

to be my Lord and Savior did my name of Judson Irwin Stone gain favor with me. I learned that from 1813 to 1850, Adoniram Judson shared the good news of Jesus Christ in Burma (now called Myanmar). I liked this fact. I chose to go to Judson College in Elgin, Illinois, which was named for him. But I did not choose it for his name or my name. I chose it so that I could get my education paid for while I bounced a ball on a court and tossed it in a hoop.

My brother Stephen and his wife named their son Judson for the role I played in Stephen's faith in Jesus Christ. Twenty-nine years later, the fact that we share the same first and last names began to play a new role in my life. That was when I took a new job where my nephew Judson worked. Because we shared the same first and last names, Judson Stone, a peer came up with a way to keep us straight: Jud I for me (Judson Irwin) and Jud M for him (Judson Mark).

Even though I am a Yank from the north, I must have a tinge of south in my words, for when folks heard me say, "My name is Jud I," they thought I said Jedi as in the *Star Wars* movies. They would frown, cock their heads, and laugh. Some would say, "May the Force be with you!" I loved this new name since it caused people to focus more on what they heard and saw from me as we talked. It was so much better than the ways people got Judson Stone wrong. Often they thought I said Judge Stone or Jedson Stone, or Jetson Stone.

Yet, Jud I does not wash all the mess down the drain. My brother David and I shared a room for two days. At the front desk, we were known as "David and Judi Stone." We both laughed — until he teased me in front of our peers. I won't room with him again.

These days, since I've found so much in my name to like, I thank God that I am called Judson Irwin Stone.

35

Just Jill

Jill Maisch

As a middle school teacher, I get to learn more than one-hundred fifty new names each year. I love one-of-a-kind names as well as names that are spelled a rare way. A few years ago, I taught two girls named Sharlette and Jaylynn. Sharlette's name was spelled that way because she had sisters named Sharlene and Sharnell. Jaylynn was named for grandparents Jayson and Marilynn.

When I was born, my parents chose the name *Jill*. I was named for no one, and my name didn't come with a cute spelling. It was just Jill. My older brother's name is *Jeff*.

As a small child I was sure that my parents chose Jill so their kids would all have names that start with J. I learned that was not the case, though, when our brother, Doug, was born.

As I grew up, I found out how rare the name Jill is.

When I was a small child, I loved the TV show *Romper Room*. At the end of each show, the host, Miss Connie, would call out the names of five or six kids she could "see" through her magic mirror. She would say, "I see Sue and Mike and Tom and Phil and Jane." Not once did she "see" Jill. It broke my young heart.

In fourth grade gym class, a boy named Jack had the nerve to choose me as his partner each time we had to pair off for square dancing. He said he did this so we could be Jack and Jill. The rest of the class thought it was great. They would laugh and say things like, "Don't fall down! Don't break your crown!" I did not find it funny at all.

Each year our family would go on at least one long trip. When we stopped at "tourist traps," I would search the stands of knick-knacks for a key chain or small items with my name on it. I'd find lots of other girls' names on them, but none with Jill.

Time after time in grade school I was asked if Jill was a nickname. I guess they thought my real name must be a name like Jillian. When asked about this, I would say, "No, it's not a nickname. It's just Jill." Deep down I wished it had been short for Jillian, though.

I think the first time I was glad to be "just Jill" was in eighth grade English when we were each asked to write an acrostic to help the class get to know us. We were to use just our first name. At that time, I did not like to write, so being told to use just our first name was, for me, too good to be true. I only had to come up with four lines while my friends Eileen, Suzanne, and Stephanie had to write more. I'm sure it took no time at all to jot down my short four-letter acrostic.

J – Joined a swim team

I – I like to go camping

L – Loves chocolate cake with ice cream

L – Likes to fish

As an adult now, I'm fine with being Just Jill. In fact, it's quite nice to have a name that's short and easy to say. I think I liked my first name most of all when I got married. Then, I went from Jill Allen to Jill Maisch. Very few say the name Maisch the right way. It's MY-sh, but most of the time I am called "Mrs. MEEsh," "Mrs. Mash," or "Mrs. MAYsh." When I hear my last name said the wrong way, I smile and tell the person, "It's MY-sh, but that's Okay. You can just call me Jill."

So, there you have it. My name is Jill. Just Jill. And these days, I kind of like that.

36
Called by Name

Verdia Yvonne Conner

Vonnie, Eeevon, Von, Evon and Eyvonne are all the ways my siblings might say my middle name — both when they were young and now. I doubt they even knew which name to pin on their big sister. With all these sounds in the air, how did I ever make sense and claim *Verdia Yvonne* as the first and next parts of my name?

With these pet names or tags, my brothers and sisters did not try to be mean. They just said what they heard year after year in the dialect of our small, southern town — a town where most adults in your young-lady life call you "girl" or "gal" as they hurled rules for norms or chores at you.

"Gal, stop all that war talk with those boys!"

"Girl, don't come out dat room 'til it's clear of the mess on yo'r bed and chest, and you put a shine on that dull wood floor!"

Even after we moved on to junior high school, some friends still used those weird tone shifts for Yvonne to get a head nod from me as we walked the halls of Robert Earl Hunt High.

Could it be that they just didn't know the right way to say the word? My best guess is that my gang of Hunt High pals were sharp and just chose to call me what they pleased. Each had her own down-south twitch and pitch for those of us who bore names with a bent that didn't fit the main set of her mouth's twangs and clangs.

By the way, in those strict-but-vital family days, my mother told me that the true way to say Yvonne was with a French twang. "If everyone says your name as 'Ya'von,'" Mother would say, "that's just the way we wanted it."

Just about the time I got that Ya'von part down pat, Verdia showed up on my legal papers. Folks didn't want to grab hold of this name. So, for a long spell I just chose not to use it. Then, I was forced to do so when I saw that it served as a gate to all types of perks that came with the use of my full name — in a search on an ancestry site or as a professional name on a business card or metal plaque on a door.

In the past, most software would allow me to use only an initial for a middle name. But "V. Yvonne" spat out as "Yvonne V.," which was not at all as I had hoped. It's even the way my name is shown on my elder credentials.

I have cause to doubt that this mess will ever end.

As my trek toward three score and ten years ticks on, I still take a post-graduate class now and then. And the teachers still use class lists with "V. Conner" on them — even after I have said, "I am Yvonne Conner. I'm on your class list as V. Yvonne Conner." I've found that when a roll call list has ten or more names, it takes three or four class dates for a teacher to get it right.

Folks may never get my name right the first time, but one thing I'm sure of. My faith tells me that God knows all of us by name: *The sheep listen to [the shepherd's] voice. He calls his own sheep by name and leads them out* (John 10:3 NIV).

This is a verse I cling to.

37

Let Me Count the Ways

Glenda Ferguson

When I took my husband's last name of *Ferguson*, I rose in the ranks . . . well, at least in the *ABC*'s. My name had been *White*, so I had been at the end of most lists. Since my high school friend had been Linda Ferguson, I could spell my new name with ease. I took on one more name, too. Since my husband's friends had given him the name "Fergie," I was to be "Mrs. Fergie."

My grandma told me that my five-times great grandfather was a Ferguson. He spent a year as a POW in the Civil War. I dug into his past but hit a snag with his war files. He was on nine lists . . . with nine ways to spell Ferguson! In each log book his name was in neat script on its own page — Farguson, Fergurson, Fergerson, Fergussson, Freeguson, Furgason, Furgerson, Furguson and Ferguson. I guess each day Grandpa would call out, "Yes, Ferguson is here," and each day a camp clerk would scan the log pages for his name, then give up and write their own ways to spell it. After a year with this stress and all the Ferguson pages, the clerks may have wished they could tell him to go home.

With help from Grandma, I found out Great Grandpa was from Scotland, where Ferguson stood for "son of Fergus, the one full of rage." I guess any Ferguson man with that short, plaid kilt blown about in the cold wind might have been real mad. The clan was not quite like the film *Braveheart*, with William

Wallace's face half blue for the last words of his war speech, "But they'll never take our freedom!" My side of the Ferguson clan, with a face all red with rage, could have a war cry like this: "But they'll never take our name of Farg…Farger…Freeg…oh, we give up! They can have it."

As a long-time teacher, I found all sorts of ways to spell and say Ferguson. When a child wrote a note or gave me a gift, a new way would show up — even though my name was in plain sight on the board. My aide would try to teach my class the right way to spell my name, but I didn't mind. I just thought it was cute.

One year Jess, a pupil new to my school, wrote my name as Mrs. Furr-guson and said my name the same way, with a high tone when she said the *RR*'s. She was not mean when she said it; that was just her voice. Even after Jess went on to the next grade, my aide would speak my name with that tone, just for fun . . . or maybe to bug me.

After many years went by, I left my job as a teacher. One day I went into an auto store for an oil change. From in back of me, I heard, "Is that you Mrs. Furr-guson?" I knew that voice! There was Jess, all grown up, now a mother with a daughter. She said, "I always remembered your name. It made me think of fur, all soft and comfy."

Now one more age group has met Mrs. Furr-guson — or at least one or two clerks in the auto store will also spell and say the name that way from now on.

38
No, My Dad Did Not Want a Boy

Kevin Louise Schaner

"*Your* name is Kevin? How do you spell it?"

"Ahhhh, *K-E-V-I-N*."

My name is *Kevin*, a great Irish name for a boy. Time for a shock: I am a lass.

Mom named me Kevin after a girl in a story. She liked the warm sound of it paired with *Louise* to go with our harsh last name, *Hoop*. Did my mom know that my whole life I would hear, "Is that your dad's name? Did your dad want a boy?" I don't think so.

Until grade two, I was the only Kevin at my school. Then my class got a new boy named Kevin Porter. It was hard not being the only Kevin; we could not tell which of us were to reply. So, I became Kevin H. and he became Kevin P. We did not know it at this age, but our first name with the *H* and the *P* would last through high school.

After we grew up, Kevin P. told me he went home after the first day at his new school and told his mom that he had a girl's name.

After Brian and I wed and we went to a new church, it was crazy. We heard a lot of, "Which of you is Brian and which is Kevin?" We had some sport with Kevin, Jr. as an idea for a baby's name. As it is, I'm sure my adult sons Owen and Neil have their own tales about, "Is your mom's name Kevin, for real?"

My job was to care for and teach young kids about books in

their school's media room. I taught boy Kevins, but never a girl one. The name plate on my desk read Kevin Schaner. I would hear the kids say, "That is not her name; that is the name of her spouse."

Many have told me that they know a girl named Kevin. I have yet to meet one, but I did come close. One day, I made a call to order books and the girl clerk said, "I'm a Kevin, too." Well, that made my day, as we went on to talk to each other the way twins would.

Sixty years along, and I still often hear alarms sound about my name. Even with a print ID card, I know to wait at check out for "the look" along with "*You* are Kevin?" I never tire of my reply — said with a straight face — "Oh, you're the first to ask." My life and my name are one and the same. It is a joy to be a lady Kevin. I know how much fun my name will yield for me and for those I meet.

I live alone now, with time to read, sew, and walk. My new way of life still leads me to meet other Kevins. After using the *Meet Up* site, I drive to local parks and join hikers. When I meet male Kevins, their jaws drop as I say, "I'm a Kevin, too. Did your mom want a girl?"

39

Names I Have Known

Mary Alice Archer

One September thirteenth, a McGowan girl was born with no name ready for her. After the first three children, Martha McGowan had been a bit stumped as to what to name her fourth child. As she lay in the hospital bed, she read a story in a magazine about a woman named Mary Alice. Martha liked the name, and her mother-in-law's name was Alice, so the name search was solved. No-name McGowan became Mary Alice McGowan.

As I was growing up, my family called me *Mary Alice* except in my toddler years, that is. Since Mary Alice was a lot to say for any four-year-old, my brother who was just two years older than I dubbed me "MaryAlley."

My father loved to give nicknames to all of us. My mother was "Baby Duck" or "Cupcake." — Why, I never knew. His children were "Jujubee," "PattyWookums," "Sepheral Q Binghongy," and I lucked out with "Mary Princess Bee Alice." He also gave us code names based on birth order and gender. My sister Judy was *K* (for kid) 1 (for first) *D* (for daughter) 1 (for first) or "K1D1." Pat was next as "K2D2," Mike was "K3S1" and I was "K4D3."

Mary was a very common name in the 1950s. In one of my classes we had four other Marys so I was happy at least to be set apart as Mary Alice. But after that year, keeping both names was a bit of a struggle. At one point, since most teachers wanted to shorten the name, I began to write my name as Mary-Alice.

In high school, while all the other cheerleaders had two-syllable names to shout — "Susan! Debbie! Vicki!" my four syllables just didn't fit into the rhythm of the cheer.

So I thought, *Should I find a cute two-syllable nickname?* One neighbor had cut it down to "Malise." Of course, that did sound the same as the not-so-nice word *malice*, so I was thankful that nickname didn't catch on.

What about "Mikki"? Could I be a Mikki?

"Susan! Debbie! Vicki! Mikki!"— that sounded great. I knew a cute, popular girl named Mikki, which drew me even more toward that name.

Then came the day when we went to the store to order our green-and-white Eisenhower High School Eagle sweaters with our names sewn on the left sleeve. After the clerk asked what name to put on the sweater, I stopped, gulped, and choked out, "Mary Alice." When it came right down to it, I just couldn't see myself as a Mikki.

At high school graduation, I heard all the formal names being read and sighed. I had no special name, just my everyday name, Mary Alice McGowan. In the past when someone asked me what my middle name was, I would often say, "Gertrude. Mary Alice Gertrude McGowan." But that was just wishful thinking.

Once I was grown, our Archer family moved to the South where two-word names were more common — "Billy Jean," "Peggy Sue," "Ruth Ann." The only hard thing I found was that many people thought my name was Mary Ellis. I got used to saying, "Mary Alice — as in Wonderland."

Yes, my name has sometimes been a trial. If someone calls me Mary Archer I know they don't know me very well. Now that I am a senior citizen, I've found that the nicknames have a place only in bygone days. The one I miss hearing most is K4D3 from my dad.

RIP Charles "Magoo" McGowan.

40

The Same Name!

Cristina Moore

My mother always dreamt she would be a mom of boys, and she had the names picked out before we were born. Much to her shock, she had two girls and not one boy. At a loss for girls' names, she thought family names would be the best fit, even though it left her few names to choose from. She named my sister *Maria Cristina* and named me, the baby, *Cristina Maria*. My sister and I were six years apart and shared the same names, if not in the same order — Cristina from my mom and Maria from my aunt.

You can guess it was hard at times to say the right name for the right kid. When one of us would act up, in a flash and in the heat of a moment, we would hear Mom yell for Maria Cristina-Cristina Maria in one breath — so she would be sure to get the right one! It made it fun to say we did not hear her or claim we thought she meant the other one. That is, at least, until she caught up with us.

To add to the same-name fun, we called my sister Cristy at home; but at school the kids called her Maria. My family called me Maria at home; but at school, the kids called me Cristina. The phone would ring in our house, and my dad would have to ask the caller's age to know whom to give the phone to.

Even though we had the same names, my sister and I were not alike. We did not have the same likes or dreams. I loved to write; she loved math. I was not good at sports; she loved volleyball. I joined the Army; she chose to teach kids. It was the same with my mom and her sister. My mom taught kids; my aunt healed the sick. My mom loved art; my aunt loved science. I guess my mom chose the chose the right woman to name each of us after.

Being raised in Tennessee, away from our family back in Puerto Rico, we had to find our own way in a strange place. Our names were our link to our place of birth, our home. As a child in Tennessee, my name was said wrong many times. My sister and I would be called Christine, Christy, or Marie; and every one added an *h* when they wrote Cristina. I would speak up when it was said or spelled wrong and tell them why it had no *h* or why it was Maria and not Marie. I would tell them that I, and my name, came from Puerto Rico, and that is the way we spelled or said it there.

As time passed we had kids of our own. My sister's kids called me Aunt Maria and my kids called her Aunt Cristy. My girls would ask why my name is Cristina at work in the Army and at home, but my nieces and nephews call me Aunt Maria. What a mess! I guess we can thank my mom for the laughs we share each time we tell the tale of Cristina Maria and Maria Cristina!

The tale goes on with the birth of my girls. My husband and I were told that we were having twin boys. He was on his way to his fourth tour in Afghanistan, and we had to come up with names for boys. We chose names of war heroes from the past. Alexander for Alexander the Great and Douglas for Douglas MacArthur.

At our first ultrasound, we were shocked to find out they both were girls, not boys. So the name hunt had to begin again. Not too long ago I found a note from my husband's second tour in Iraq in 2004 when he went across the sea on the USNS *Bob Hope* with all the unit's gear and trucks. In the note he sent me he said we would name our first child after this great man for all his help in the past.

So when we had our girls, one was named *Hope*. (She may be the only eleven-year-old who even knows who Bob Hope was.) The other twin was named *Helena Marcela* after our Grandmothers.

Helena's name is often said wrong, just like mine. She tells them no, she is part Puerto Rican and it is Helena Marcela, after her grandmothers. New names and a new time, but the same story.

Only my sister and I can imagine how much worse it could have been.

At least I didn't saddle twins with different versions of the same name!

41

The Top Ten Things About Being John Leatherman

John Leatherman

#10: No, I'm not related to him.

#9: Yes, I'm sure. My great-great grandfather came from Germany with the name *Lederman*. His scions would Americanize it in different ways at different times. So I have second and third cousins with names like Laderman, Letheman, and Lethermon . . . but not that one.

#8: My dad never had to spell his name over the phone. He'd just say, "Leatherman. It's spelled like it sounds." Since I live in the era of a famous talk-show host, I can't do that.

#7: In college classes, a hushed silence would ensue when my professors would call on *David*. And Lettermen Hall, where some of us guys lived, was named for the student athletes who stayed there when it was first built. But still my dorm mates thought I was the son of a rich donor.

#6: When my sister, Anne, wed, she had no qualms about dropping the name Leatherman for Cox — since it made her name a total of only eight letters, even with her middle initial. On the other hand, my wife, Marinilda, had to drop her middle initial just to get her new name to fit on a credit card.

#5: No, I'm not related to any of the famous Leathermans.

#4: Yes, there are famous Leathermans, like Russ Leatherman. You might not know his name or his face, but you may know his voice, at least if you liked to go to the movies before 2014. For all those who didn't carry around the movie page of the local news, Russ Leatherman was the full, deep voice behind the words, "Hello, and welcome to MovieFone!"

#3: There's also Tim Leatherman, inventor of a line of multi-use tools that bear his name. We may not be related, but at least if I ever buy a pair of pliers that can also drive screws, scale fish, open cans, crack nuts, and tell me which way is north, it will bear my name — with no added fee.

#2: While I'm not angry that I don't see any money from the use of my name on a commercial product, I just hope there isn't a Leatherman for plumbers that fix toilets. I'd hate to think that you can buy a John Leatherman.

#1: The number one thing about being John Leatherman . . . Sorry, State Farm insurance agent John Leatherman of Greensboro, North Carolina, I just renewed my domain name again!

42

The One Who Called My Name

Kellie Zeigler

The sound of your name from a loved one's lips can reach not only ears but also deep into the soul. What we're called is more than just a word; it is a sign of who we are. Each cell joined into this one form — a name holds the place for each of us on the earth. That's why a name has so much weight. It is who we are and speaks to each part in us and the whole of us at the same time. If we are blessed then we have heard our name called in a way that brings us joy to hear it.

My name is *Kellie Rae Zeigler*. I'm fond of it, though I could be biased since it is my own. I'm sure God knew my name prior to my birth but to my mom and dad, Kellie came out of thin air. Rae was a gift from my Mom to make a one-of-a-kind name. It came from the name of my Mom's grandfather, Ray, a man I didn't know. For the most part, I think of my name only when I hear someone else say it. In school I had to wait to hear, "Kellie Zeigler," since it was at the end of roll call.

Of all the times my name has been said, two stand out.

When I was a child, I heard my name called — in a voice that seemed soft yet was loud in the sense that it couldn't be missed. "Yes, Lord," I said. "What is it?" It was a call to Him, a call to be home. All on my own, I prayed and took His gift to heart. I did not know what was next, but I knew I'd strive to take His path while He led the way. Yet, as I grew up, I spent less time in His

Word, and the path began to stretch out. It wasn't too wide, but just a bit was too much for me.

My name began to be called by ways of the world that vowed to give me tons of words to fill my mind. I thought I'd be smart with what I learned in all these books. But since I had set His book to the side, I did not know that the world's words were mere fluff that puffed up my sense of self.

Mine was a slow drift — a book here, a book there, a phrase that seemed to be good since it talked of Jesus and love. But these views were not based in the truth. I had let the world come into my heart, and I had not yet seen that what I was up to was sin. God should have been the main focus of my life, and it pains me to say that He was not. I thought I was in search of the truth, but I had been caught up in the lies of those who claim we each have our own truth. If I had kept His book by my side and read from it each day, I would have been able to tell with ease what is true and what is false.

Thank God I heard my name called one more time — soft at first, like a light knock at the door. Each rap grew in strength 'til I couldn't tune it out. At this point I fell to my knees and prayed, "Lord, forgive me for all those times I turned from You. It is not what I want. I want to do Your will, not mine. Please take me back and show me how to do it right this time."

I learned that it's a huge task to choose whom to heed among those who call our names. It feels good to hear your name, but we can't make our choice based just on how it feels. Some calls are good and right; some seem true but are quite wrong at their core. I had to retch when I saw that like Eve, I'd been tricked by a voice that seemed good but was false.

The truth is, God did not leave me. It was I who was blind and could not see how close He was to me. It was I who had grown deaf to the sound of my name.

Thank God, He kept at it and it was not in vain.

The Lord, our God, who was, is, and will be is The One I want to call to me. When He calls my name, I come to life and am filled with peace.

May we all hear the call, the sound of our own sweet names. We can take the gift, repent, and walk in the way of truth so one day we may know that, as the old song goes, "When the roll is called up yonder, I'll be there."

And in that final roll call, I won't care if my name is last.

43

Not Me!

Penny Cooke

My husband's fever was 102.5. We had just come home from the doctor with his meds for strep throat. He was glad to get back on the couch when we heard a knock on the door — a very loud knock. I threw open the door to find three cops. One was a friend who stood there with a pained look on his face as he asked, "Penny, is Harry here?"

"Yeah, he's sick on the couch. Why, what's up?" I asked as I let them in.

"I'm sorry, but we have a warrant for his arrest."

What? I guessed that's why our friend's face looked so pained. He had to do his job, but he knew Harry and so also knew it didn't seem right. Not *this*.

"Whatever for?"

By now they stood in front of Harry as one told him, "Harry Cooke, you are under arrest for armed robbery and attempted murder of a police officer."

Whaaat?

After they read him his rights, two of the cops went to the bedroom with him to keep their eyes on him while he got dressed. Then they cuffed him and led him — fever and all — to one of five cop cars. Off they sped as lights flashed, sirens shrieked, and neighbors gaped.

Shocked, I didn't know what to do . . . at first. Then, since I had to stay home with our baby son, I called my dad who knew most of the cops in our small town. He went to the station to find out what he could. He was able to see Harry in the cell and asked him, tongue in cheek, "So, did you do it?" Now Harry was the one with the pained look on his face.

The warrant was from a town south of us, the place where my husband should have been taken. But our local cops knew that the other town's cops would beat Harry up, so they vowed to hold him until the other cops could come to ID him. Eight hours later, the officers showed up with the driver's license of the suspect. For sure it had my husband's name and address, but the image was not his. My husband was able to place the man as someone he knew from work, and he gave them his real name.

It turned out the guy got his hands on my husband's wallet at work and stole his name and ID. He then went on to commit an armed robbery and shot a cop who then shot back. The wound had sent the suspect to the hospital, which told us why some hospital bills had been sent to our house. He had snuck out of the hospital and was on the run when they came to get my husband.

At last my husband was freed to go home — where he was even more happy to be back on the couch.

Though at the time we were quite stressed, over the years we've laughed at the great story it's made. He had just about earned the name, Dirty Harry!

44

My Name to Claim

Barbara Farland

"Fear not, for I have redeemed you; I have called you by name, you are mine."

Isaiah 43:1 ESV

Most girls who play with dolls love Barbies. The fact that I shared my name with that belle of our daily play gained me fame all through elementary school.

"Hi, Barbie!" cried my chums as I walked into class to hang up my coat.

"Barbie, come sit with us," begged groups both here and there as I crossed the cafeteria with my lunch tray.

"There goes Barbie," sang out the crowd as I hopped on the bus with a wave.

This is truly how my days went as a young child, and I liked it. What's more, I got used to it. Who wouldn't? I knew the high life well and had no cares in the world.

But when I turned twelve, the main goal of most — if not all — of us kids was to grow up and grow up fast. My plan? I felt the need to shed the likes of Barbie. In short, it pulsed with "cute" while I craved to be cool. The thing is, what I was left with let . . . me . . . down.

Barbara. From my teen years on, I didn't like my name. To me, it felt plain. It felt cold. It felt old and worn out. What's more, it's the near twin of words that call bad things to mind —

words such as *barbarian*, *barbed wire*, and *barbiturate*. On top of that, Barbara doesn't bring to mind any thought linked to charm or smarts or any trait of great note. By its very best definition, my name means "strange" or "foreign." Yes, it could have been worse, but in my book as a young girl, that was bad enough.

Strange. Foreign. I blamed *Barbara* for my changed lot in life. As hard as it was to face at the time, the name fit me quite well as a teen. I was born into a blended family — two halves made into quite the mess of a whole. With a foot in both camps, I seemed to live at the heart of all of the feuds and fights between my parents, and among my sisters and brothers.

Yet I was raised much like an only child, and I felt most at ease among books and yarn and hooks and thread. Sure, I did have a few real friends, but nights alone in my room took up most of my time. So, all in all, I did feel strange and foreign. With all it implies, my name made sense for me.

After high school, came college, then my work life. Over time, Barbara left its grim mark on my career too. With twenty-five years in business communications under my belt, I liked the field. I was good at it, and I planned to stick with it until the very end. But with the rise of social media and all things virtual — when web hits and page views gained ground, and words seemed to lose their heft — my job began to feel flat, bland. Dare I say strange? When it came down to it, I just had to find a new way. So I hired a life coach, bought some books about faith in the midst of change, and hoped for the best.

In my search for next steps, I took a walk to the park one morning, my Bible tucked in my bag. My goal? To find a bright patch of grass where I could spread my things out, read, pray, ask, and seek. It wasn't long before the Lord led me to scripture that not only was spot-on for the task at hand but also speaks to the issue and power of names.

You see, God reminded me of the true name He gives to each of us: *Beloved*. But at the same time, He showed me how our earthly names can show good sense, too.

My name of Barbara took on a new cast through the lens of the Bible. In Deuteronomy 14:2, God says we are set apart. In Romans 12:2, Paul writes that we are not to conform to the pattern of this world. And in Colossians 3:2, Paul goes on to say our minds should be set on things above — a choice the world deems quite odd.

In a flash, my heart came to know and love my name through the light of God's Word. All at once, I was struck by what a gift it is to be strange and foreign. In fact, my sad and flawed view of my name changed to sheer joy! I began to see myself the way God sees me: His Barbara.

Abraham. Sarah. Peter. Paul. And me, Barbara.

On that warm summer day, I joined the ranks of those who have donned new names — names by which God wants us to live and grow, to thrive and serve. So, today, I claim the name Barbara with pride. I claim the name Beloved with joy and thanks. And I praise the name of The One who knows me through and through, and calls me His own.

45

Lucky Dog

Lin Daniels

For months my niece, Jen, begged her Mom for a puppy. In fact, that was her only wish for her twelfth birthday! But there was an issue; some folks in the family were allergic to dogs.

My sister took Jen to a pet store where they spoke with the owner about a trial run. Jen fell in love with a jet-black miniature schnauzer. The six-pound pup went home with them for a few days. The family would name the pup *Lucky* — if she got to stay. The pup would be lucky to find a new abode, and the family would be lucky to adopt a furry friend.

After two days with nary a sneeze, wheeze, or itchy eye in the house, Lucky had a real home!

Even though Lucky was a dog, she had the nine lives of a cat. On Valentine's Day, she found a way to gorge on a whole box of chocolates and was still okay. One time she ate a box of crayons. For a week she had multi-color poops! But she lived on.

Her real test came at the age of seven when she had a very large tumor in her tummy. (Yes, we *did* pray for her.) After the vet took the tumor out, he gave us only a twenty-five percent chance that it would not come back. But Lucky beat the odds. And from then on, we used her story to bring hope to many a human who faced cancer.

Lucky had ten more years of a good life. Every time she saw the vet, he would note, "Lucky has truly lived up to her name!"

46

A Name That Fits

Alice H. Murray

Hale is the last name with which I was born. You don't get to pick your birth name, but mine is spot on to tell about me, my family, and my life.

One of the Middle English words that the name *Hale* comes from is *Hæle*, which means "hero." A true patriot, my dad was in the army in World War II and was proud to often fly the flag at home as well. Some of our family claim that one of our forefathers is the great Revolutionary hero Nathan Hale whose last words on the way to be hanged for spying are said to have been, "I only regret that I have but one life to lose for my country." My brother was a career Marine who also loves the U.S. Thus, he named his son Nathan Hale.

Hale also comes from a word that may mean a home near a salty water body. Aha! Mom grew up on the coast of South Carolina. Every summer we went to Pawley's Island to spend a week or two at the beach and visit our relatives. I was in kid heaven when I could swim in the Atlantic Ocean, put my toes in the sand, look for a shell, chase crabs, and play with my cousins. Where else would a Hale want to relax and have fun than by the sea?

I am a word nerd. I love to learn new words and think on how to use words and how two words can sound alike but not be spelled alike. That love has served me as I found new ways to play with my name. Since I grew up in Atlanta, it was rare to see snow, but we did have hail. Cool — a weather event that bore the sound of my family name!

Name that tune! It's "Hail to the Chief." Again, a word like my last name in sound but not in how it is spelled. The title and the idea of government made me think. And I had it so much in my mind that I chose political science as my major in college. Later, I went to work at the Georgia State Capitol where I was with those who ran the state. Hail to those in power in the Peach State!

But then I left to go to law school at the University of Georgia. In one odd way, the first week of class was fun. Since *Hale* is short and easy to say, every professor called on me first to stand up and reply to his query about the law. Even if it wouldn't have been my choice at the time, later I was glad to get a scary part of law school — the first time I had to stand and recite — over with right away.

When I got a ring on my left hand, those in my law-school class began to ask if my last name would be hyphenated. Uh, no. I wasn't going to take the chance that in the mouths and ears of those who lived with me in the South *Hale-Murray* would sound like "Hail Mary." So, once a wife, my last name was Murray. But I was still a Hale. That name just moved in front of my new last name and after my first name — with no tiny line to join Hale and Murray.

As my husband was in the Air Force, we soon had to move to Ohio, which was far away from my family in Georgia. It was fun to go back home and see the family. All of us being in the same place was a big event. Every time, we would be happy and silly and say, "Hale, Hale the gang's all here!" After all, we were the Hales, and we were there as a group.

Time has passed, and I'm now a Mimi. Even though my grandchildren bear the last name of their father, I must stay "hale and hearty" if I'm to keep up with them. This Mimi plans to be at all their soccer games, have them spend the night at my house, and enjoy fun times with them in other ways.

Even if I could go back and change my birth name, I would not do it. The name Hale fits me to a *T*. The word can mean many things, and some of them tie into what I have done in my life . . . and like the word, I can be more than one thing. I am Mom, Mimi, a lawyer, and a writer. Hail to the name Hale!

47

The Only M

Mary Lou Redding

A girl named Kimberley taught me how big a deal a name can be. She and her family lived on our street. The mom was Patti, the dad was Paul, and Kimberley's little brother was Paul K. When they learned that a third baby was on the way, Kimberley began at once to lobby about the baby's name. "Please, please, please name the baby a *K*. Everyone else in this family is a *P*. I don't want to be the only *K*!" When her brother was born on New Year's Day and named Kyle, Kimberley was over the moon. Not being the only one whose name began with *K* made her feel as if she were more a part of the family in some way.*

Not being the only *K* meant more to her than I would ever think it could. I mean, what's in a name? And then I thought of my own family.

My next two older siblings were Darrell and Dorothy, and my next two brothers were Danney and Donnie. When I asked the story of my name, Mother told me she had planned to name me Dana, to fit in with the others. But when I was born my dad said my name had to be *Mary Lou*; he wouldn't hear of any other, and so Mother gave in. Like Kimberley, I took notice that my name made me the odd one out. Though I'm not sure it had to do with just my name, I never felt as if I fit in with my family. I wasn't "one of them." I felt like an alien. (And bathed in the *Star Trek* myth, I even dreamed that I might be one — which my brothers were happy to agree with. They also told me I was adopted, to make me feel even more left out.)

After I became an adult, my mother told me the rest of the story of why my dad chose that name for me. My father could never stay true to just one woman. All through the years, he had "friends" on the side. And his paramour at the time of my birth was a woman named — you guessed it — Mary.

As I look back now, I have to think that Mother may have pulled back from me on some level (or many) when she found out why my dad named me as he did. She and I were never close. Frost hung in the air between us at all times. I thought it came from the fact that she and I were so *not* alike. All of my life and hers, we were at odds about *every* thing. But maybe it had to do at least in part with my name. Maybe when she heard it or saw it, she couldn't help but think of that woman and all the other "other women" — and the pain my father had caused her over and over.

If that is so, I can look at Mother with grace. Over time, I have learned that what we feel is not a choice. What we feel, we feel. And what we say, the other one hears from what they feel. We may not seek to bring harm, but our words can hurt. When we use an easy label or speak too soon, we may wound. We may open a door to old pain even though we do not know it. Our words can draw others close or wall them out. Paul wrote to the Ephesians, *[Let] your words . . . give grace to those who hear* (Ephesians. 4:29 NRSV). So when I see hurt in the eyes of some person as I speak, I search for the word of grace that should come from my lips next.

And I am called to offer that grace to myself, too. When I cringe at the sight of some person or pull back or turn away for no cause that I can name, maybe it comes from a scar or old wound deep in me. With time, as we open more fully to the

Holy Spirit's work in us, all of our wounds can be brought into God's light to be healed. We can be free of their hold on us. We can change to be able to love more fully, to offer grace more fully. May it be so.

*Kimberley is now married, with three kids of her own — and their names do not begin with the same letter.

48

a boy named ed

Ed Sanabia

There once was a boy named ed
Born with two hands ten toes one head.
But alas much to his shame,
The lad had no middle name.
Such a dirty little shame —
No middle name,
No middle name at all.
He might be either up or down
Lost or found
Fox or hound —
In all without ballast or frame.
One name short
was his bane.
The boy with no middle name
No middle name at all.
Though all did end well,
As sure as there is heaven and hell
Start and end
Foe or friend
Let there be middle —
Be it a piddle —
Let there be middle for all.

49

Oh, for a Name's Sake!

Jorja Davis

Jorja is not a usual name. But most of the time — and once people get it — my first name rings with joy in their ears.

Mama and Daddy's tales of how that name came to be did not match up. Mama always told the story this way: "Your daddy took me to Amarillo in his Model A Ford to see the movie *Whistle Stop*. One of the actresses in the movie was Jorja Curtright, a hometown girl. When we chose your name, I thought it was the best possible way to spell it because any place you went in life, it would make you one of a kind."

Daddy, who often told me I could tell people he was a smart aleck, told it this way: "When the nurse came to have your mama fill out your birth certificate, she was sleeping, so the nurse gave it to me. I stood there, with my pen in the air. Hmmm, G-E-O-R-G-I-A — that is a lot of letters for a little girl to have to learn to spell her name. So, I wrote it just like it sounds on the certificate, J-O-R-J-A."

One way or the other, that's the way my name is spelled. Later it morphed into a new form. Since my little sisters would tend to blame everything on me, once when one of them wet her diaper, she told my mama, "Dorda did it." That name stuck; from then on I was *Dorda* at home. And to this day when anything goes wrong, both my sisters still say, "Dorda did it."

When I got to go to school, it was back to Jorja. I admit that at times I wanted it to be usual like my friends Elizabeth, Meredith, and Eleanor; but then again, my name was not as hard to spell.

Sometimes I just plain hated my name. It seemed to mix up everyone. Anywhere I've lived, people find a wrong way to say it. When I lived in Illinois, it was "Yorya." When in Texas, it was "Horha." Anywhere I went, folks would also find a new way to write it: Jorgia, Jorga, Georjia. Somewhere along the line, I learned to make sure it was on paper (now computer) list and then to spell it out loud before I said it. That way, once they "get it," then even though they may forget who I am, they always know my name.

I've never met a girl (or boy, in fact) with my name. So I did grow up to feel like one of a kind, even though sometimes that made me feel as if I were too small to see. Then one day, my girls and I caught a bus on the way back from play in the park. We sat on the back seat. Three stops later, a teen girl stepped on in a Burger King uniform. There on her name tag was my name – *Jorja*. I got so wound up that I dug in my purse to show her my school ID and driver's license. I jumped out of my seat and moved to where she sat, my two girls trailing along. By the time we got up to her, I was babbling. I must have scared her to death since at the next stop, she ran off the bus — miles from any Burger King. After that I might hear of folks named Jorja, but none of them ever came across my path.

Years later we moved to Georgia to be near one of our now-grown daughters and our small grandchildren, George and Meredith. I often heard, "Jorja and George (yes, that is my husband's first name) moved to Georgia to be near George." What a hoot! Will I never hear the end? By the way, can you think what comes about when people in Georgia try to spell my name?

As I grew older, I hoped a child or grandchild would be named after me. It never came to be. Then, just last week, I went to the doctor's. The med tech who took me back to see the doctor was making small talk. She said she had a new puppy at her house, a pit bull, and they named her Georgia. Before I left the office, she came back with a big smile on her face and told me, "I've called the vet and told them my pit bull's name is spelled just like yours."

It seems I got a namesake after all!

50

Lover of Peace

Rhonda Dragomir

I am the only *Rhonda Dragomir* in the world. I've Googled it. No one else shows up in the search.

The last name I was born with was not so rare. *Johnson* took up five pages in our hometown phone book — back when we all had one. My first name reached peak use in 1958, the year of my birth, so I did meet a Rhonda here or there over the years. Still, I seldom found things etched with my name in the rest-stop gift shops. One time, I found a Rhonda bell, though, even spelled right with an *H*. I prized it for years.

Then I married Dale Dragomir. Oh, help me. I had to morph from Rhonda Johnson to "Rhonda who?" When it was my turn to see the doctor, nurses who paged "Mrs. Jones" or "Mrs. Smith" opened the lobby door and called, "Rhonda?" I didn't wait for clerks to ask me to spell my last name. I just said, "Rhonda Dragomir, D-R-A-G-O-M-I-R."

When we took a trip to Romania, the land of Dale's kin, no one thought my name was weird. Our friends took us to Viştea de Sus, a small town in Transylvania where "all the Dragomirs are from." I preened, even in the days before vampire books were in style. One of our hosts said, "'Is good Romanian name," and told us it means "lover of peace." *Draga* means *dear* or *lover*, and *mir* means peace.

I am a meek soul, so it's not hard for me to live at peace. When I first read a verse like Psalm 34:14, which tells us to *turn from evil and do good; seek peace and pursue it* (NIV), I had never sown strife, so the words did not prick me. After I learned what my new last name means, I yearned to bring peace more often. When thanked as I helped people patch up their relationships, I would reply, "Yes, Dragomirs love peace."

Then God gave me a real test when my pastor husband, Dale, and I were forced — based on lies that cleaved my heart in two — to leave a church we had served for more than twenty-three years. The false words cracked me open, and what oozed out was not peace. I craved a sword so I could hurt those who had hurt us, and I schemed ways to do it.

Before I could act on my wrath, I felt nudged by a Bible verse about who I am in Christ — a trait etched in my last name. *If it is possible, as far as it depends on you, live at peace with everyone,* Paul wrote in Romans 12:18 (NIV).

When we moved, I needed a new driver's license. I signed my name, and as my pen formed *D-R-A-G-O-M-I-R,* pain like a knife pierced me to the core of my being. What would a lover of peace do when faced with my crisis? I knew, even though I did not want to do it. I vowed to walk a new path, though it would not be easy.

I worked to truly forgive those who had lied. I turned from my need to make war with words. I met false claims with truth said in love. I prayed for those who cursed us, and then I spoke blessings over them. I dived so deep into the sea of peace that I've never come up for air.

I did not choose my name. God chose it and used it to forge me into a woman who loves peace and seeks it.

51

The Title I Adore

Becky Alexander

When I worked with kids as a children's minister, my name changed from *Becky* to *Miss Becky*. I loved it and even used "MSBECKY" on my auto license plate. On any given Sunday, no fewer than one hundred high-pitched voices would call out that title; along with it came hugs to my legs and tugs on my sleeves.

In the kids' minds, the name put our best church volunteer in an iffy spot. What should they call the husband of Miss Becky — "Tim?" "Mr. Tim?" "Mr. Alexander?" One girl solved the issue when she dubbed him, *Mr. Becky*.

Years later, a burly man with a young child walked up to me at Walmart and said, "Hi, Miss Becky."

I had no idea who he was.

"I'm sure you don't know me, but I know you. As a small boy, I would often visit your children's church. We played games and ate lots of snacks." He laughed. "And you taught us about Jesus."

I can tell you, Miss Becky's eyes filled up with tears, and her heart spilled over in joy.

While I talked to the man's son, I caught a glimpse of the new generation that needs the love and grace of Jesus. So, the title I adore won't change back to just Becky any time soon. There's much more work for me in this world. I will pray these words to the Father above:

Even when I am old and gray, do not forsake me, my God, till I declare your power to the next generation, your mighty acts to all who are to come.

Psalm 71:18 NIV

52

Not Short and Not Sweet

Jean Matthew Hall

My parents blessed me with the name *Joyce Aliene Jean Matthew*. It caused problems in school for twelve years. Every person in my family calls me Jean. But schools would insist on Joyce. Did you know that schools like to have neat files? Their files had to be neat, and their files kept grades by your last, then first name. First — as in Joyce.

Each year of grades one through twelve, we had to change my files in the school office from Joyce Matthew to Jean Matthew. Even so, I still had to tell each class teacher that my name was Jean.

You'd think the word would have spread from one staff to the next, wouldn't you?

No. Files are files. Names are a big deal for files. School staff are slaves to files. Thus it went from year to year.

For all three years of high school those in charge of the files mixed up my records with a girl named Joyce Matthews. Though I did not know her — and she did not know me — I sure knew all of her grades — and she knew all of mine.

But my name woes didn't end with high school. They trailed with me five more years through college. The most chaos came when I changed from one school to the next — three times. It seems that colleges are slaves to files, too.

While I fought with schools due to my name, I found new ways to add to the mess. I learned to drive. You know those small cards that we have, the ones that give us the right to drive on roads? Yeah . . . those. They don't have room for four names. So, my name changed to Jean Aliene Matthew.

But wait! I got a part-time job. That gave the IRS and SSA access to my files and my name. And Social Security said that on their card I must use my legal first name — Joyce. After that I had two cards with names that didn't match each other.

Then came pay checks and a bank. I held my breath to see which name would be in my bank's files.

There's more! I found a husband. Yep, I was a wife with a new name — Joyce Aliene Jean Matthew Hall. Try to say that in one breath or fit it in one blank.

Now I was known as Jean Matthew Hall.

Do you get how big of a mess this was?

For forty plus years, life went well with my name as Jean Matthew Hall. Then — the Patriot Act was born. No big deal for me at first. But . . .

I moved from North Carolina to Kentucky.

That began a steep grade of tough steps to climb:

- I had to buy a new plate for my car.
- But first I had to get a new driver's license.
- Before that, I had to get new insurance for my car.
- Before that, I had to have three forms of ID with the same name on them.
- To do that I had to make the names on my birth certificate and my Social Security Card match.
- To do that I had to go to court to change my legal first name. (I got rid of the Joyce part.)
- Then I had to ask for a new Social Security card to match my new birth certificate.
- Then I could get a new card.
- Then new insurance
- Then the new plate

The whole deal took five months. But, at last, I could say that I was in line with the laws of the State of Kentucky — that is, until I was stopped for my speed and had to tell all of this to the man with the badge.

Arg!

The moral to this story is this:

Parents, please stop and think. Then, name your kids. Sheesh! Think about school and that your child must learn to write and spell their name!

Think about the things that will come as your child grows up!

Think about those cute small kids and mean teens who will tease your child for his or her odd or strange name!

Yes, *Be Kind* to your kids. Give them names that will not cause shame or pains with files and cards and grades in school.

Your kids' names are for their sakes — to be a joy in life — not for your fun or jokes or grandfather's heritage.

Please!

Signed with hope for your kids,

Jean Aliene-Matthew* Hall

*which Social Security says must be one name

53

Take His Name

Patricia Tiffany Morris

My father and my mother dear
Named me with a kind of cheer.
With initials that spelled P.A.T.,
My name formed my identity.

Patricia is my given name,
But Patty was my first nickname.
And Pat became my college glee:
Patricia Ann and Tiffany.

At school I had a bright strong mind,
But I was teased with rhymes not kind.
Like Patty, Ratty, Fatty Cat —
Mean words that sting with hurt like that.

I wasn't fat but could not thwart
When kids would lie and tease for sport.
I hid my tears and played their games,
Yet could not change or shake those names.

The words they hurled would taunt and tease.
Their prose would bring me to my knees —
Those boys who'd sit and spit at me
Or girls who'd chit and chat with glee.

When one boy's hate was bold to tease,
And one girl's gait mocked mine with ease,
I felt my heart would shrink and weep.
At times I could not eat or sleep.

Yet kids that caused my heart to sting,
Brought pleas for grace, gave pause to sing.
For God created all of me —
My gait, my weight, and heart to see

That He would be my all in all.
He knew me while I grew so tall.
So nix the blame and nix the shame
For names we cannot fix or tame.

I'll sign my art with Tiffany —
A mark so bold that all can see.
And when it's joined to my husband's name —
Of Morris — then can I set my aim

To give all praise to Christ our God,
Who says our days are never flawed.
I'll take my name and not place blame.
I'll claim my fame in Jesus' name.

The end of rhyme and poem draws near.
I'm sure the goal in time shines clear.
What's in a name is like pure gold —
A hope and joy that we might hold.

God makes us strong to stake our claim.
Let's share in song and take His name.

About the Authors

Becky Alexander (p. 121) teaches for the International Guide Academy and leads tours across the U.S. and Canada. Before her travel adventures, she taught kids about Jesus for 25 years as a children's minister. Now, she volunteers with Operation Christmas Child.

Becky's devotions appear in Guideposts' *Pray a Word a Day, God's Comforting Ways,* and *In the Arms of Angels.* "Connected by Kindness" in *Chicken Soup for the Soul: Miracles & Divine Intervention* received first-place awards from Carolina Christian Writers Conference and Southern Christian Writers Conference. She has contributed to three *Short and Sweet* books.

Becky collaborated with her biologist brother and teacher sister to write *Clover's Wildflower Field Trip,* a colorful children's book filled with scientific facts and vocabulary words. Now, she's working on *Clover and Critters in the Creek.* Say "Hi" to Becky at HappyChairBooks.com.

Mary Alice Archer (p. 93) has worked in education for over 40 years. For the last 26 years she has taught middle schoolers math, English, history, French, art, drama, and science. Now she is tutoring Chinese students online.

She has a B.S. in Exceptional Education from the University of Central Florida and has written and illustrated the award-winning children's book, *If a Cat.* In addition, she has published in Focus on the Family's *Clubhouse Jr.* and in two previous editions of the *Short and Sweet* series.

A Southern California girl for the first 40 years of her life, she then moved to Central Florida. She and John have three children, six grandchildren, two Havanese dogs, a Bourke's parakeet, and a Hermann's tortoise named Melville, of course.

Patty Barry (p. 48) belongs to the tribe of storytellers. Words have always felt important to her, whether spoken or written. She loves to read and write poetry, short stories, and even commercials. The rhythm and sound of words have always brought her joy, whether she or someone else has written them.

An avid reader herself, she tries to instill a love for reading and storytelling in children that she meets. She especially enjoys helping her grandchildren find good books to read, and then discussing them together to hear their views on what they've read. She also coaches high school debate students in speech writing and delivery to help them to find their own voice and to express themselves with clarity and confidence.

Susan Brehmer (p. 28), an encourager and Bible enthusiast, believes treasure is found in the Word of God and that time with Jesus sheds light on Scripture. She loves to lead others into worship and through the life-changing Word of God.

Susan supports her fellow travelers on their trek through the Bible and had fun crafting a ten-minute summary of the Old and New Testament as a souvenir of their journey together.

Her violin students give her welcome opportunities to refine her motivational speaking skills. Susan is also grateful to friends and mentors who saw the writer in her before she did. Host of the *Encouraging Voice Podcast*, she writes worship songs and devotional articles for the *Christian Journal* and *Pathways to God*. She can be reached at www.SusanBrehmer.com.

Gene Burgess (p. 66) has been married to Kathy, his high school sweetheart, since 1978. They have five children — three of a kind (boys) and two of another kind (girls) — a full house and a growing flock of grands.

He has been self-employed since college, first in full-time Christian service as a pastor. For the past 30 years he and Kathy have operated a sign business.

Gene believes that what we do occupationally cannot be separated from what we are. So he strives to be genuinely himself in all his dealings. Gene especially enjoys sharing principles from his book, *21 Ts to a Triumphant Life,* in which he offers a model for experiencing life triumphantly. Gene prays that his words will inspire his audience with a new passion for living.

Frank Caudle (p. 50) pursued a B.A. in Theology and an M.A. in Education. Since then, oral communication has been part of his everyday life as he has taught both in the classroom and in the pulpit. He has also served as an Academic Dean in a Bible College where he taught the Life of Christ for 12 years.

Since that time, he has served different churches for 25 years. From the perspective of his broad background, he is now focusing on writing, speaking, and serving as a ministry consultant.

To fine-tune his writing, Frank belongs to *Richmond Christians Who Write* and a writers' critique group. He also writes for a number of publications.

Rev. Verdia Yvonne Conner, EdD (p. 87), is a retired Elder with the East Ohio Annual Conference of The United Methodist Church. Her active years of ministry included roles as pastor, district associate of missions, and three terms with the Board of Ordained Ministry.

Yvonne has a passion for families impacted by social issues. She developed a community-based academic program to assist families needing support for their suspended students; she volunteered with AmeriCorps as a reading tutor and volunteered four years on the inaugural Cleveland Community Police Commission. Her philanthropic pledge includes funding an endowment granting scholarships to persons committed to community service.

Yvonne is an aspiring writer, winner of a Writer's Digest 2020 Poetry Award, and host of *The Forgiveness Project: How's That Working for You?* podcast. She can be contacted at vyvonnec@outlook.com.

Penny Cooke (p. 103) is an award-winning author, Certified Biblical Life Coach, Bible teacher, and speaker. Her passion is for people to be in the Word and prayer and to be empowered by His Spirit for this battle we call life.

Penny's book, *Pursuing Prayer – Being Effective in a Busy World*, won first place in the Bible Study category for the 2020 Selah awards. She is a contributor to Worthy Inspired's *Let the Earth Rejoice* devotional and Lighthouse Bible Studies' *Heart Renovation* Bible study. She has written articles for CBN.com and Thoughts-About-God.com and has had two columns published in *Blessed Living* women's e-nagazine. Penny also enjoys encouraging her blog readers at pennycookeauthor.com.

Penny and her husband live in sunny Florida and have three grown children and seven fun grandchildren.

Yolando Cooksey (p. 35) is a mother, and most importantly, a daughter of God. Continuing her journey of healing and restoration, Yolando has earned her Bachelor of Arts in Psychology and *Mindset Life Coach* certification, and is currently working on a *Master Life Coach* certification as well — all to fulfill her God-given purpose of reaching the lost.

Life experiences have taught Yolando many lessons. She hopes to inspire, motivate, and encourage others to connect with God — mind-body-spirit. Yolando is a published devotional author with *The Upper Room*, a contributing author to *The Short and Sweet of It: When the Right Word Is a Short Word*, and a co-author in the anthology *Arise From the Ashes*. Yolando is currently working on her next book, *Living Your Best Life Golden: The Essential Guide for Finding Balance in Your Life*.

Lin Daniels (p. 108) retired from teaching physical education for 40 years — all but one year in elementary school. She and her twin sister are avid golfers. When playing as partners, they agree on which identical clothing to wear but choose one item (usually a hat) to be different.

Recently, Lin has found a passion for pickle ball – a game similar to tennis but played on a smaller court while using a whiffle ball. Her other interests include writing Christian devotions, working with youth at church, and on occasion, preaching. Lin gives thanks to God for the depths of His love as well as all the surprises He has graciously bestowed on her.

Jorja Davis (p. 116), a retired teacher and librarian, taught in the classroom, at church, in her private piano-and-voice studio. She and her husband have two married daughters, Chariti Young and Josi Lane, and three grandchildren, Elan, George, and Meredith.

For 26 years George (Bill), her husband of over 50 years, was in the United States Air Force. After he retired, they lived in Texas for 15 years then moved to Georgia where their youngest grandchildren, George and Meredith, lived. There she had a private studio where she taught piano and voice until her retirement. Now she writes prayer liturgies and studies, essays, and articles, and she hopes to someday unearth the novel hiding among the UFO's (unfinished objects) in her computer. Mostly she enjoys time with family and friends.

Diana DiMaggio (p. 81) is a retired attorney and a real estate and securities investor, trying to recover from decades of multisyllabic brain-drain. Although a serious student in Susan King's class at a Christian writers conference, she had no time for the "short and sweet" homework assignment, there. To her amazement, once home, she found short words to be a therapeutic, soothing brain massage — enabling her to finish her short-word homework and submit it late.

Last year, Diana moved to Texas to walk beside her 93-year-old mother on her journey Home. Diana is in the final editing phase of her first book, *An Extraordinary Ordinary Man*. While it reads like fiction, it is the biographical journey of her 10 years of marriage to the man she was not looking for but whom God knew she needed.

Rhonda Dragomir (p. 119), a multimedia creative who treasures her fairy tale life in Central Kentucky, insists her home is her castle — even if her prince refuses to dig a moat. She has published works in several anthologies and periodicals and is seeking publication of her first novel.

Rhonda has garnered numerous writing awards for both fiction and nonfiction, including her selection as 2019 Writer of the Year by Serious Writer, Inc. In 2020 she was a finalist in ACFW's Genesis Contest for her first novel, *Destiny Delayed*, a 16th century historical romance set in the Scottish/English borderlands. She is currently researching and writing an historical novel set in Kentucky during the Civil War. You can view her published works and read excerpts of her works in progress at www.rhondadragomir.com.

Susan Engebrecht (p. 7) has written for newspaper columns, magazines, and anthologies, including *Chicken Soup for the Soul*. She co-directed a Christian writer's conference, and also taught at writers' and women's conferences. She's won several writing contests including the Jade Ring. Trophies from her Toastmaster contests require dusting every now and then as well.

When Susan isn't writing, she's sewing or breaking glass. Bits and pieces of fabric become quilts. Glass is soldered into catchers of light. But teaching is her passion.

Her husband, Keith, has been a consistent support and doesn't mind being called "Knight" in her writing or even out in public. She is thankful for two grown sons and their families who are her delight.

An adorable puggle makes sure she gets out of the house for fresh air, to mingle with neighbors and to collect fresh ideas.

Barbara Farland (p.105) has spent most of her career in business communications and creative writing. In addition to leading countless corporate campaigns, she has contributed to various anthologies, including *Chicken Soup for the Soul, Cup of Comfort, Christmas Traditions, Hugs,* and *The Talking Stick.* Beginning in 2019, this all gave rise to her leading a weekly writing group for accelerated elementary students at FAIR (Fine Arts Interdisciplinary Resource) School in Plymouth, Minnesota.

Barbara serves as a lesson writer with Study.com, a language arts instructor with AoPS (Art of Problem Solving) Online, and a tutor with the AVID (Advancement Via Individual Determination) program of Robbinsdale Area Schools. She enjoys working with students and other teachers through deep conversations, encouragement, teamwork — and of course, writing. She makes her home in Minneapolis with her husband Terry and daughter Nina.

Glenda Ferguson (p. 89) obtained education degrees from College of the Ozarks and Indiana University. After a career as an elementary teacher, she started writing, with encouragement from the Writers Forum of Burton Kimble Farms Education Center. Her work has appeared in *Angels on Earth, Chicken Soup for the Soul, Mules & More, Reminisce, Sasee* and other publications.

The Indiana Arts Commission has included her poem "The Buffalo Trace Trail: Then and Now" in the INverse Poetry Archive. Glenda writes devotionals for animal lovers and for the Ladies' Prayer Circle at her church.

As a volunteer with Indiana Landmarks, she conducts tours of two historical hotels in southern Indiana. Glenda and her husband, Tim, live on an acre in Paoli, Indiana, which they share with Speckles the cat and a variety of wildlife visitors.

Desiree Glass (p. 41) has written for numerous publications and websites including *Guideposts, Short and Sweet Too, The Short and Sweet of It, Angels in Disguise?, A Joy-Full Season, Pen in Hand, Connections, Dragonfly, The Times-Crescent* newspaper, and her church blog.

Currently a high school career and technology education teacher, Desiree has 30 years of experience teaching all ages from infant to adult. She earned her M.A. at Notre Dame of Maryland University and her B.S. at Salisbury University. She is active in her church — serving as trustee, greeter, and leader of a women's small group. She is the mother of three adult children and grandmother of ten. In addition to spoiling the grandkids, Desiree enjoys kayaking, hiking, and life on the farm. Her blog can be accessed at http://desireeglass.blogspot.com.

Kelly Godzwa (p. 33) serves with her husband, Dave, as missionary to Mexico with Assemblies of God World Missions (AGWM). Life in transition is their present "state of being." Kelly enjoys learning new things, making connections, challenging herself, and expressing her thoughts in written form.

While starting her career as a high school Math teacher, motherhood became her primary focus as her family grew. Her future goal is diving deeper into the Enneagram and exposing others to its benefits as a growth tool. She is most at peace outdoors in God's amazing creation but does her best to create a peaceful space wherever she goes. The family currently lives in Missouri, with three adult children in college and a 12-year-old mini schnauzer.

Jean Matthew Hall (p. 123) lives in LaGrange, Kentucky with her old-lady dog, Sophie, who naps while Jean writes. Jean's poems, stories and articles have been published in a variety of magazines and anthologies. When not enjoying time with family (eight gorgeous grandkids) and church, Jean is immersed in children's picture books — reading, studying, reviewing, and writing them. Her first picture book, *God's Blessings of Fall*, was released in September 2019. Her second picture book is set to release in 2022.

Jean is a member of the SCBWI, Word Weavers International, Write2Ignite and the Kentucky Christian Writers.

You can learn more about Jean at her website and blog www.jeanmatthewhall.com. Find her on FaceBook at Jean Matthew Hall Author and on Twitter at Jean_Hall. Check out her Boards on Pinterest at JeanMatthew_Hall.

Mary Frances Heitzman (p. 44) is a past president of the Minnesota Christian Writers' Guild. She lives in Bloomington, Minnesota with her husband, Duff, who grew up knowing all of his grandparents.

As she was growing up, Mary often imagined what it would be like to sit on a grandparent's knee to ask them what life was like as they were growing up on farms with no cars or tractors, and only horses or oxen to plow the ground. She longed to ask what it was like to grow up without electricity.

She fondly remembers stories from her mother about reading the newspaper to Grandpa Grommesch, who was nearly blinded by measles when he was a child, and how he walked to town on Saturday nights and brought home a bag of candy for the children to share.

Leah Hinton (p. 10), based in Texas, is a poet, short-story author, screenwriter, and playwright. Among her awards are the McClatchy Fiction Prize for her stories *Blue*, *Dark Fog*, and *Spin-Me, Charlie*; the Poet's Prize for *Barefoot* (Dallas Area Writers), and the Audience-Choice Spotlight Award for her play, *Ripe* (2019 Stage Writers Festival).

Her play, *Paper Thin*, was a feature selection by Imprint Theatre in 2020. Her short films *Lost Man*, *Bantam*, and *Single* were in production in 2021 as part of the feature-length anthology, *Dad-Father-Papa*, from Carpe Diem Pictures. She is a full member of the Dramatists Guild, Associate Director of Stage Writers, President of the Writers Guild of Texas, Event Liaison of the DFW Writers Room, and founder of R.A.W. Arts Poetry Guild.

Doris Hoover (p. 52), can be found somewhere between the Sunshine State of Florida and Sunrise County, Maine. Most likely, you'll find her outside collecting ideas for her writing. Her love of God and nature inspire the devotions she writes.

Doris is a mother of three and grandmother of five. She and her husband, Tim, enjoy traveling to visit their family.

Doris has won awards for her devotions. In addition to being published in *The Upper Room*, CBN.com, *Arise Daily* e-devotionals, and *InkspirationsOnline*.com, Doris is also a contributor to many compilations such as *Arise Daily to Peace*, *Short and Sweet*, *Light for the Writer's Soul*, and more. Her first book is *Quiet Moments in the Villages, A Treasure Hunt Devotional*. You can visit her website and blog at ANatureMoment.com.

Penny L. Hunt (p. 78), award winning author, speaker, and blogger, has been published in *Chicken Soup for the Soul*, *Guideposts*, *The Upper Room*, almost every edition of the *Short and Sweet* series, and online in *Just Eighteen Summers*. Her most recent book, *Bounce! Don't Break . . .* helps others bounce back from setbacks. *Little White Squirrel's Secret — A Special Place to Practice*, is an Amazon.com bestseller children's book dedicated to her severely autistic granddaughter.

Penny lives in the rural-peach-growing region of South Carolina with her husband, Bill, a retired career naval officer and attaché, and their two dogs. While she enjoys gardening and gourmet cooking, her greatest passion is to lead others to a personal and intimate relationship with Christ. Visit her at PennyLHunt.com.

Liz Kimmel (p. 53) has published two books of Christian prose/poetry and a grammar workbook for middle school students. Her work has appeared in all books in the *Short and Sweet* series. Her devotions are included in several of Guideposts' *All God's Creatures* daily devotions and in their *One Minute Devotions*.

Married for 42 years, she and her husband, Cary, have two children and four grandchildren. She earned a B.A. in Elementary Education at Bethel College in Arden Hills, Minnesota, and currently lives in St. Paul, Minnesota.

Liz serves as administrative support for three non-profit ministries — Great Commission Media Ministries, MN HOP, and Minnesota Christian Writers Guild. She has retired from her position in the front office at her church and is excited to see what projects the Lord will bring to her in the coming season.

Rita Klundt (p. 13) became an author, speaker, and story collector after 30 years as a registered professional nurse. Her first book, *Goliath's Mountain*, tells a poignant and tragic love story, giving readers a view into the heart of a woman touched by mental illness and suicide. Rita's passion for true and transparent stories has led her to collect more stories than she can write or tell in her lifetime. She collaborated with 26 of her friends to compile and publish the first in a series of books, *Real Life Real Ladies: Short Stories from the Pew*.

Rita and her husband live in central Illinois. They enjoy travel and are excited about where this stage of life and story collecting is taking them. Connect with Rita or watch for more great stories at www.ritaklundt.com.

Debra Kornfield (p. 26), always intrigued by the mysteries of human expression, was born in Guatemala to missionary parents. During 20 years of mission work in Brazil with her husband, Dave, and four children, Debra published several books and wrote for *Cristianismo Hoje* (*Christianity Today*) and popular *Lar Cristão* (*Christian Home*). She pioneered abuse recovery, breaking taboos through her award-winning book *Vítima, Sobrevivente, Vencedor* (*Victim, Survivor, Victor*). Her ministry GAVS (support groups for survivors) continues today under Brazilian leadership. She framed her memoir *Karis: All I See Is Grace* (now in Spanish and Portuguese, too) around her daughter's luminous journals and poetry.

Debra enjoys her grandchildren, hiking, keeping up with seven sibs, and doing most anything with Dave. Learn about her historical fiction series at HorseThief1898.blog. Follow her personally on ButGod.blog.

Linda L. Kruschke (p. 71), recovering lawyer and sexual-assault survivor, writes candid memoir and fearless poetry and delves into hard issues others tend to avoid. She aspires to show women that God's redemption and healing are just a story away. She is the author of two self-published poetry books, *Light in My Darkness: Poems of Hope for the Brokenhearted* and *Rejoice! Rejoice! Poems for the Holidays*, available on Amazon.

Linda blogs at *AnotherFearlessYear.net*, *AnchoredVoices.com*, and *BrokenBelievers.com*, and has been published in *Fathom Magazine*, *The Christian Journal*, *Bible Advocate*, *iBelieve.com*, *WeToo.org* blog, *The Mighty*, *Calla Press* literary journal, the *Life, Repurposed* compilation, and several anthologies. She is editor of *Swallow's Nest* poetry journal of Oregon Christian Writers. One of her stories will appear in the December 2022 *Christmas Cats* compilation from Revell.

Billie Joy Langston (p. 31) is a journalist and freelance writer of inspirational and positive-living literature. She is also a Christian Hospitality Specialist who conducts hospitality ministry workshops for churches and faith-based organizations. She earned an undergraduate degree in anthropology/journalism, and a Master of Education (with honors) from Howard University. She also attended Capital Bible Seminary.

Her publishing credits include anthologies in two Guideposts books, *Miracles Do Happen* and *In the Arms of Angels*, in addition to *Chicken Soup for the Soul – I'm Speaking Now*. Devotional publishing credits include Wesleyan Publishing House, Cross River Media, and ChristianDevotions.us. She writes opinion editorials and human-interest stories for a variety of regional newspapers.

Billie enjoys sharing her knowledge of the written word and providing career counseling to traditional and adult students.

John Leatherman (p. 98) is a writer, editor, cartoonist, writing-contest judge, word-puzzle creator, and escape-room designer. He is a longtime member and former officer of Word Weavers International, where he is a writing mentor, leads occasional seminars on self-editing, and writes a long-running grammar blog. He has won numerous writing awards from Word Weavers International, American Christian Fiction Writers, and other organizations. He has worked with over a dozen authors to edit, proofread, rewrite, and revise their manuscripts for publication. He also served as Communications Editor for Recode Media.

His writing credits include book reviews for *Christian Retailing*, scripts for Shoestring Radio Theater, devotionals for *Keys for Kids*, and cartoons for several magazines. He maintains a secret identity as a mild-mannered software consultant who lives in Florida and has two kids and a dog.

Allyson West Lewis (p. 29) is an award-winning author specializing in speculative fiction. After over 20 years as an Institutional Director on Wall Street and a Business Developer for an IT networking company, she returned to her childhood love — writing. She's written a fantasy novel, a dystopian science-fiction novel, and has published blog posts, short stories, and articles in literary magazines and anthologies.

For many years, Allyson taught parenting for desperate pre-teen parents, facilitated leadership training, served as a one-on-one mentor, and led a ladys' small group.

She pursued her lifelong passion for horses and enjoyed having her own farm. Now she's turned to the wonderful world of tennis.

She loves her amazing husband, sons, and grandchildren. Allyson writes from Roswell, Georgia with a golden retriever and one irascible terrier sprawled at her feet.

Terry Magness (p. 69) is an author, speaker, and founder of Grace Harbour Ministries, a biblically-based teaching and discipleship ministry to women of the nations. She writes for the Southern Missouri District Council's *Refresh* blog for credentialed women and pastors' wives, and has authored two books.

Terry loves people and is passionate to help them know God and mature in Christ, and through Him, overcome the many challenges to victorious Christian living. Her experience as an ordained Assembly of God minister, which included years in biblical study, pastoral counseling, mentoring, and — more recently — coaching, have well equipped her for this calling.

Terry enjoys writing, photography, art, nature, travel, and fishing with her husband, Don. She and Don treasure their family — daughter, Valarie, and son, Greg, and his wife, Jean Anne, and their three amazingly gifted granddaughters.

Jill Allen Maisch (p. 85) and her husband, Bill, reside in a Maryland suburb of Washington, D.C. They are fortunate to live just 15 minutes from her 93-year-old mom and within a short drive of their six adult children and their families. For the past 43 years, Jill has thoroughly enjoyed teaching middle-school science, but looks forward to retiring after the 2022-2023 school year.

When she's not teaching, Jill enjoys writing, camping in their new RV, riding her e-bike, and traveling. Her passion is leading cross-cultural mission experiences and, as chair of the Church and Society group at her church, she is actively involved in addressing social-justice issues that impact her community.

Jill has had ten devotions published in *The Upper Room,* and her writing has appeared in four previous editions of the *Short and Sweet* series.

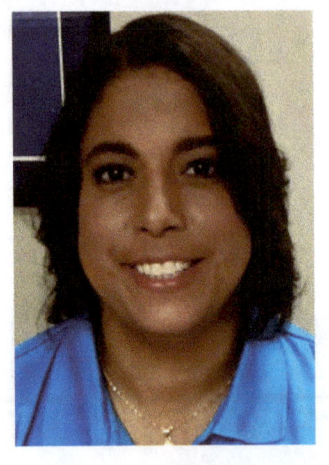

Cristina Moore (p. 95) was born in Puerto Rico and grew up in Tennessee. Currently, she lives in North Carolina with her husband of over 20 years and her 4 children: Tripp, Katie, and twins Hope and Helena. She is the owner and CEO of Bronze Star Homes, an employee at Duke Energy, and currently serves in the North Carolina National Guard as a Colonel, Chief of the Joint Staff.

Cristina celebrates God's Word by sharing the grace and miracles both she and her husband have witnessed through multiple combat deployments and their call to serve their community and country.

In her spare time, Cristina places family as a priority and is enjoying returning to her passion of writing and touching the lives of those reading her words.

Patricia Tiffany Morris (p. 126), an incorrigible writer, passionate artist, and eclectic creative, sketches ideas in her sleep — that is, when she takes time to sleep. All-night reading and studying served her well during architectural design studio at ISU in the 80s.

Now an empty-nester, she's inspired by her rhyming husband, who reads her suspense-filled fiction in delightful character voices and helps her brainstorm sticky situations. Patricia actively supports fellow authors and offers geeky tech services. She owns Tiffany Inks Studio LLC and branded JOURNALING SCRIBBLES™, a collection of artsy journals, notebooks, and planners.

She adores Pinterest and hashtags but finds Twitter quirky.

Her goal to share Christ through inspirational fictional stories brought her numerous awards from 2019-2021 in poetry, short fiction, children's stories, and suspense fiction, including 1st Place at BRMCWC for her upcoming split-time novel.

Alice H. Murray (p. 109) is an adoption attorney who has practiced law in Florida for over 30 years. She is an officer and board member of the Florida Adoption Council and of Hope Global Initiative. While being a lawyer is her profession, Alice's passion is writing. She was a staff writer for adoption.com and has had pieces published in several *Short and Sweet* books, in *Chicken Soup for the Soul*, and in the *Northwest Florida Literary Review*.

Alice has written for legal professional magazines, her local paper, a missions magazine, and various online sites. She particularly enjoys writing devotionals and sees teaching lessons everywhere. In her "spare" time, Alice volunteers teaching an ESL (English as a Second Language) class for foreign-born residents in her area, a joint ministry of several local churches.

Suzanne Dodge Nichols (p. 39) grew up in Gulf Breeze, Florida where during a high school composition class she discovered the rewarding discipline of writing. Through the years, she has found creative expression in almost every genre of the printed word. She especially enjoys blending words and art in ways that can both delight and challenge the observer.

Suzanne is published in seven books of the *Short and Sweet* series, a co-author of Volumes 1 and 2 of *COFFEE with God*, a contributor to *Day by Day: 40 Devotionals for Writers & Creative Types*, and is a 2021 Selah Awards recipient.

Suzanne makes her home in Hartselle, Alabama with her husband of 45 years. They have three children and nine grandchildren who live *much* too far away.

Julie Ann Payne (p. 18) is a speaker, an encourager, and a teacher at heart — passionately inspiring women to grow in their faith through one-on-one discipleship and Bible study. She has authored the book, *Strong Women Cry Too: A story of hurt, heartache, and healing*, under the pen name Julia Margaret in honor of her mom.

Having lived on both coasts of the United States, it is fair to say she loves to evaluate and compare perspectives in life . . . and this carries over into her writing.

Julie, a member of Word Weavers International, is a seasoned floral designer, a blessed grandmother, and a devoted lover of fried ice cream. Butterfly aviaries and floral gardens inspire her. You can visit her website at www.juliamargaretauthor.com.

Shelley Pierce (p. 46) and her husband, Tommy, raised their four children in the foothills of the Great Smoky Mountains of East Tennessee, and now enjoy the gift of grandchildren. Tommy is the senior pastor of Towering Oaks Baptist Church, and Shelley serves alongside him on staff as the director of preschool and children's ministries.

Shelley understands the challenges today's children face. She enjoys the friendships, laughter, and even the struggles of ministering in the lives of kids. She believes every experience presents an opportunity to learn more about God's great love.

Her publishing credits include middle-grade fiction series *The Crumberry Chronicles*, *Sweet Moments: Insights and Encouragement for the Pastor's Wife*, several picture books, devotionals in *The Upper Room* magazine, and several pieces in the *Short and Sweet* series.

S. E. Pruitt (p. 21) is the oldest of six children, all of whom won the lottery by getting a set of parents who valued church, education, and cookies. She grew up in the San Francisco Bay Area and now lives in nearby Salinas. The fourth of five generations of teachers, she taught middle school for about 30 years.

She wrote and privately published a couple of family histories and has a short story in the 2020 summer issu of *Woven Tales*. Since retirement, she has worked on three novels of historical fiction.

She enjoys volunteering at her church, learning from her writing groups, having high tea with friends, and spoiling 14 great-nephews and great-nieces, who all have a mad passion for gummy bears.

Mary Lou Redding (p. 112) is the fourth of seven children. Her parents were authentic Kentucky hillbillies involved in an actual shooting feud into their early adulthood. One of her grandfathers was a coal miner, the other a moonshiner. She's part of the first generation of her family to be born outside Kentucky since her ten-greats-grandfather George Gideon Ison arrived in Letcher County in the early 1700s.

Retired Editorial Director of *The Upper Room* magazine and one of the creators of the *Meeting God Bible*, she lives in Brentwood, Tennessee, just far enough from her child and grandchildren to keep them from dropping in unannounced. Mary Lou's latest book is *God Was With Me All Along: A Guide to Capturing Your Memories and Telling Your Story*.

Jeanne Roberson (p. 63), the oldest and only girl out of eight children, was born in Springfield, Massachusetts and grew up primarily in Florida. Most of her adult life has been spent between Rhode Island and Florida, where she currently resides with her husband, Bob, and their Maltese, Bengie.

She is a retired real estate agent, cancer survivor, and Red Cross volunteer who has a powerful love for Jesus. She has a grown son, two beautiful adult daughters, and is Grandma to a precious little girl.

Jeanne began writing in 2016 after attending the Blue Ridge Mountains Christian Writers Conference. She developed the inspiringsouls.com website and is presently working on her biography. Besides Jeanne's love for writing, she enjoys fishing, gardening, volunteering, and most of all spending time with her granddaughter.

Martha Rogers (p. 56) is a southern girl who loves sweet tea and all things chocolate. She thrives on encouraging others to discover true joy and freedom in the richness of God's unending grace and mercy. The mother of two grown daughters adopted from China makes her home in Alachua, Florida with her husband, Doug.

Her other passions include singing, painting, photography, entertaining, and decorating. With a background in community theater and a degree in Music Education, Martha currently directs a group of ladies called Sweet Notes who sing monthly at local nursing homes. She believes being young at heart is the only way to live, loves to travel, and hopes to add a wild-west adventure to Utah as a favorite destination soon.

Ed Sanabia (p. 115) is a native Californian who has been writing for over 40 years. He primarily considers himself a playwright, having written many plays and skits for Christian theater. But, Ed has also dabbled in the world of short stories and poetry.

After an encounter with Jesus of Nazareth, his motivation and priority changed. He was drawn to write pieces that would not only entertain but touch, move, and cause people to reflect and consider truth. Ed was determined not to simply write embellished "gospel tracts" but to try to create literature that would draw people to heaven. It has been a fascinating journey, and he is especially grateful for the chance to work, laugh, and at times weep with the actors who bring his plays to life.

Bill Sanner (p. 38), a real renaissance man, is gifted, involved, and busy. His first book, a memoir of his days riding a submarine in the US Navy in the 70s, won an Author of the Year Award in 2016 from the Artist Music Guild. While he has owned several tech companies for decades, he's also the Chairman of the Board of Directors of Malaika Orphanage in Uganda, and is the President of his local Rotary Club.

For over a decade, Bill has been a featured performer in the large variety show, *The Spectacular Senior Follies*. He plays eight instruments and is an accomplished musician with a published CD, having written more than 100 songs. He also composes and arranges original music for large concert bands. His motto is "Let's have some fun and do some good."

Kevin Schaner (p. 91), a retired school librarian, is also a writer and speaker. Personal essays in her book *Dinner by Candlelight: Comfort and Joy for Advent*, encourage readers to initiate conversations about how we celebrate Christmas. The celebration may change from year to year, but Christ remains the same.

Global missions ministry is one of Kevin's passions; she has journeyed to Africa 10 times with United Methodist Volunteer in Mission teams. Her articles in *Response Magazine* report on additional relationship-building experiences through United Women in Faith. Every day she practices Spanish on *duolingo* and has recently learned to strum a baritone ukulele. With her grandchildren, Kevin hikes all four seasons on the North Coast and loves living in multicultural Cleveland Heights, Ohio. Kevin can be reached at schanerkevin@gmail.com. (See also "Acknowledgment," page 155.)

Xavia Arndt Sheffield (p. 15) has written music, lyrics, comedy, poetry, devotionals, and a Bible Study titled *Life Principles from the Women of Acts*. Her devotionals have appeared in *The Upper Room, These Days*, and online for the Washington National Cathedral for Advent and Lent. Her writing has also appeared in *Monday Morning* and *Presbyterians Today* magazines.

As a Presbyterian minister's wife of 40 years, Xavia has been involved in most aspects of church life, including teaching Women of the Bible and other classes, creating Sunday School kickoff programs, serving as Children's Music Director, and crafting over 1,000 bulletin boards. She holds a B.A. in Music and an M.A. in Speech/Theater from SDSU She and her husband have a daughter and a son.

Judson I. Stone (p. 83) is a volunteer at the Walton Correctional Institution Florida, a Bible study leader, and an amateur photographer. He has retired as a pastor, corporate chaplain, and Fellowship of Christian Athletes volunteer sports chaplain.

His biography of his father, *A Last Chapter of the Greatest Generation,* was published in 2016; he has also published articles and poetry. He has completed a book about his son's tour of duty in Iraq and transcribed his great uncle's World War I diary. His current project is editing a manuscript about his great-great uncle who died as a young missionary in Oman in 1899 while serving with the Arabian Mission.

Judson is married, the father of three sons, and has been blessed with five grandchildren. He and his wife reside in Santa Rosa Beach, Florida.

Wilma Vernich (p. 58) writes from the perspective of a mother of two and a farmer's daughter. Learning on the knee of her father and through Scrabble games with family, Wilma went on to study Journalism in college — infatuated with the power of prose. Although she has not written her book yet, Wilma often expresses her innermost yearnings through poetry and her desire to encourage people through her meditations for *The Upper Room.*

In addition to baking homemade bread, Wilma can claim the old-fashioned love of writing letters and sending them through "snail mail." She lives outside Nashville, Tennessee where she can see pretty sunsets and loves to be outside — whether it's working in the yard, waterskiing on a lake, or riding her bike.

Candice Weathers (p. 60) lives in Nashville, Tennessee where she was born, reared, and stayed — at least until 2022. Happily married to Monty, one of the best barbers in town (although she won't let him cut her hair), Candice enjoys gardening, DIY projects, Star Wars and Marvel movies, crocheting, reading, and cooking carne adovada.

She works a little more than part-time as a process consultant for an IT company, and in her spare time helps build her husband's barber shop empire or snuggles with her furbabies — Boston Terriers named Charlie and Max. Her newest ventures include planning a move to the wild wild west of New Mexico, dabbling in the fine art of sourdough baking with her starter named Flo, and maybe writing more after she takes that Spanish class for real this year.

Kenneth Avon White (p. 23) resides in Gastonia, North Carolina. His business career centers around equipping anxious employees to successfully adjust to workplace changes. Ironically, in the world of writing Ken finds that change is welcomed. Plots and characters and places all adjust to an ever-changing landscape as stories unfold like a yellow brick road that leads to some place magical.

Several of Ken's devotionals have been published in *The Upper Room* magazine. He is also published in several *Short and Sweet* anthologies. Ken volunteers at his church, gets lost on weekends driving down country roads, and has watcheed way too much Netflix during these pandemic times while mentally rewriting the scripts or wondering if God is speaking to him through an actor on television. A big focus for Ken right now is losing his new COVID weight.

A. DiAnne Wilson (p. 73) was born in East Tennessee. Now, after 34 years of seeing the world through her flight-attendant travels, she is relishing this new-found experience of feet-on-the-ground life at home that she shares with her husband, an amazing music man, in the foothills of the Great Smoky Mountains National Park.

She loves singing, writing poems of faith and nature, working on DIY projects, and vice-chairing a black-bear-cub rescue. As a Southern Appalachian naturalist, she daily marvels at the artistic revelation of our Creator's mind on glorious display in the great outdoors. As a believer, she aspires to grow, to share the truth of God's Word, and to extoll the greatness of the glory of God's grace in every way that she can find.

Kellie Zeigler (p. 100), an observer of life, enjoys collecting these observations in the form of articles, memoirs, poems, and fiction. Her favorite place to be is outside, soaking up the sun and reveling in God's creation. She originally started writing to get all of the words out of her head, but soon found they just kept coming. Now she keeps a notepad and pencil tucked away in each room for whenever inspiration strikes.

Her crazy dreams fuel her fiction, and she's grateful for the experience of over-the-top emotions that underpin her prose. She seeks to help Christians make choices in everyday life that lead them closer to Christ.

She hopes people will find comfort in her words and that God's glory may be seen throughout her work. You can find her at kelliezeigler.com.

Susan Cheeves King

Compiler and editor of the *Short and Sweet* series, Susan Cheeves King (susankingedits.com) offers editorial services that include editing (nonfiction books, novels, devotionals, articles, and more) and also mentoring. While serving 24 years as an editor for *The Upper Room* magazine, she began teaching at what not totals over 100 Christian writers' conferences in the U.S. and Canada.

Her professional life has also included 27 years of teaching English and feature-writing classes at Lipscomb University, Biola University, and Abilene Christian University to over 4,000 students. Early in her career, Susan served as a book editor and radio-program producer/on-air talent, wrote magazine features as a freelance writer, and functioned as a seminar facilitator in leadership and group dynamics.

Susan and husband, Joe, live in middle Tennessee and have three grown children, two grandsons, and two foster grandsons.

Acknowledgment

Our special thanks to Kevin Schaner (p. 91) who suggested the name for the *Short and Sweet* series.

www.ingramcontent.com/pod-product-compliance
Lightning Source LLC
Chambersburg PA
CBHW070448090426
42735CB00012B/2488